THE TRUTH ABOUT LEADS

Revealing little-known secrets that focus your
lead-generation efforts, align your sales and
marketing organizations and drive revenue

by
Dan McDade

Information in this book is based on professional experience of the
author. This book is intended to provide insight based on this
knowledge, and represents over 20 years of experience contacting
hundreds of thousands of prospects on behalf of scores of clients.

FIRST EDITION

ISBN-978-0-9830267-0-9

Published by Onsei
www.onsei.net
Printed in the U.S.A.

"*The Truth About Leads* lifts the fog of confusion about why most lead-generation efforts fail or fall short. It's an easy read and its principles are practical and actionable immediately."

– Brad Childress, Executive Vice President of Sales, nuBridges

"*The Truth About Leads* is a terrific book that zeros in on one of the key issues facing business today—how to nurture a lead through the sales funnel and convert it into a customer. If you're interested in turning leads into dollars, this book is for you."

– Jamie Turner, Author, *How to Make Money with Social Media*;
Chief Content Officer, 60 Second Marketer

"The way customers buy is changing profoundly. This mandates changes in the way marketing and sales engage and develop customers. Leads that translate into qualified opportunities are at the core of the new engagement strategies. Dan McDade vividly demonstrates the failure of traditional lead-management processes, focusing on how marketing and sales collaborate to produce better results. *The Truth About Leads* is a call to action for all sales and marketing people to focus on quality rather than quantity. It provides a clear path to align critical activities to produce the best result."

– David Brock, President, Partners In EXCELLENCE

"When I worked with Dan, he was famous for plain and honest straight talk. His book follows that same route—with insightful information presented in a clear, no-nonsense fashion. Companies smart enough to listen will get what amounts to an expert consultant for the price of a book."

– Bill Husted, Nationally Syndicated Technology Columnist

"Continuous successful lead generation is the lifeblood of any business. Dan's slim volume provides a proven methodology to revive your lead process. These are simple truths, discussed with total clarity. Learn the truth about leads now and watch your business grow to new heights."

– Rich Bohn, Executive Editor, SellMoreNow.com

"Salespeople involved in today's high value, complex sale will find Dan McDade's book provides great ideas on how marketing and sales can work more closely to increase revenue and close more deals! This book provides solid, practical advice that both marketers and professional salespeople can immediately use and apply."

– Stephen J. Bistritz, Ed.D., President and Founder, SellXL.com;
Co-author, *Selling to the C-Suite* (McGraw-Hill 2010)

"It begins in the foreword, by stating, 'It describes what **management** must do…,' continues through Dan's preface where he succinctly states, 'This book is for **C-level executives**, **vice presidents** and **directors**…,' and ends only with the final chapter, 'always speaking to **upper level management**.' The key to driving greater results in sales always starts at the top. There are too many books written by and for the producer, but Dan not only skips the sales popularity contest, he writes from research and best practice—he tells sales and marketing leaders and coaches what they need to hear, not necessarily what they want to hear about driving sales.

"*The Truth About Leads* is a great example of how one needs to step back and analyze what is being done. Sales leaders are typically working at warp speed and outside of a weekly or daily dashboard review, not enough time is dedicated to continuous improvement, to analyzing how they can drive more revenue. There are only so many levers sales or marketing executives can pull and leads are not only the foundation for the sales process, but understanding and affecting how you obtain, qualify and solve their problems is totally in your control. I guarantee you will make some changes after reading *The Truth About Leads.*"

– Bill Eckstrom, President, EcSELL Institute

"I've known Dan McDade for many years, and without question I consider him one of the leading authorities on developing and scaling a high-performance sales organization. Dan knows that it's not just about sales—he addresses the key issue of creating a closed loop and fostering continuous improvement in the cycle and relationship between marketing and sales. The bottom line is that *The Truth About Leads* is the type of must-read guide—focused on both strategies AND tactics—that senior executives can use to help them succeed in these challenging markets."

– Chris Selland, Independent Analyst, Focus; Former Yankee Group Analyst; Founding President, The CRM Association

"I was pleased to read that Dan McDade has distilled the engagement principles culled from his years of lead-management experience into a comprehensive overview. He is a dynamic voice in one of the most important areas of business success: quality lead generation. The information Dan puts forth in *The Truth About Leads* is consistent with what our research on relevant marketing ROI metrics shows is best-in-class and will help any organization improve its business performance."

– Chris C. Houpis, Senior Analyst, Marketing Strategy and Effectiveness, The Aberdeen Group, a Harte-Hanks company

"I don't recommend that which I have not read. I read Dan McDade's book because there are few books just about leads; about the dos and don'ts. For a small book, this is packed. It is not self-serving tripe. I like his road map for improving lead generation and business development. He makes a case for generating fewer leads and what doesn't work when it comes to lead management. There is a powerful review of direct marketing basics (worth it alone). Yes, there are commandments (my words) for improving lead generation. There are eight in-your-face chapters to guide the most serious lead-generation/management managers. Buy at least three copies. The whole team needs to read this."

– James W. Obermayer, CEO, Sales Lead Management
Association; Author of two sales lead management books

"Dan is a true pioneer in the lead-management space and *The Truth About Leads* is a great way of sharing his experience and perspective with business executives. While the concept of pursuing fewer prospects may be contrary to the instincts of sales professionals and marketers, Dan's book presents this compelling case through research as well as real-world client examples. I'd recommend this book to any company that is re-thinking its pipeline approach."

– Andrew Gaffney, Editor, *DemandGen Report*

"As the title of this book suggests, your sales, marketing and management teams need to be able to handle the truth before they can hope to fix any lead-management issues. Dan McDade cuts right through the B.S. that so often divides marketing and sales, reminding us that leads are a moving target. *The Truth About Leads* is a must-read to learn not only how to identify quality leads but also how to keep up with them for more closed sales and higher profit. But ask yourself first: Can you handle the truth?"

– Hallie Mummert, Consulting Editor, *Target Marketing*

"I've got a lead for you. Get this book. Read it. Follow what Dan says religiously. Because this dude truly gets lead generation unlike anyone I've ever read. He knows not only what the value of a lead is but how to measure that value. He knows why the gap between marketing and sales hurts the ability to get leads—so he deals with that too. He understands that all leads are not created equal, so he shows you which ones matter. In other words, Dan McDade is the man to listen to if leads are important to your sales process. If they aren't, you're probably no longer in business. If you are, though, get…this…book. Now."

– Paul Greenberg, Author, *CRM at the Speed of Light*, 4th edition

Dedication

I dedicate this book to my associates at PointClear. Thank you for all you do for PointClear and for the millions of dollars in revenue you generate for our clients. I also dedicate this book to Jeff Fisher. Jeff is a true friend who hounded me night and day until the book was done. Finally, I dedicate this book to my wife, Nancy. Without her cheerful disposition and tireless effort, this book would never have been completed.

Table of Contents

Foreword: Jeff Fisher, Partner, Hi Tech Partners

Achieving business excellence—lasting, sustainable excellence—is not easy. It is, in fact, hard—very hard. Although there are many different approaches to the pursuit of excellence (programs, seminars, webinars, books, and tools of all kinds), one approach hardly ever works in all cases. We still must take the time to sort it out for ourselves and select the bits and pieces that work for our business.

At Hi Tech Partners, we have attempted to help our clients create the right business models for their organizations. We have worked with them to integrate a variety of best practices to take their businesses to the next level. In those efforts, we have borrowed and adopted from many sources and used the most appropriate ones to improve the overall performance of our clients.

In our pursuit of marketing and sales excellence for our clients, I was introduced to Dan McDade, the founder of PointClear. PointClear is a prospect development firm in Atlanta, Georgia, and does business throughout the United States.

My initial reaction to PointClear's claims of a better way was, frankly, "Ho hum, there are lots of folks trying to do this, but no one can do it better than those businesses with a committed in-house lead-generation and business-development effort."

I was wrong. Very, very wrong. PointClear does indeed do it better today than the vast majority of both outsourced and in-house efforts.

PointClear brings expertise, commitment, structure and methodology to lead generation and business development that have proven to be absolutely essential to business success in today's ever more competitive global economy.

What makes PointClear different? There are at least three important reasons:

- PointClear takes a strategic approach to planning for lead-generation and business-development efforts that accelerates time-to-benefit.
- PointClear employs experienced, business-savvy professionals to engage appropriate-level prospects.
- PointClear's advanced multi-touch, multi-media, multi-cycle process multiplies results.

We have been recommending PointClear to our clients and friends for more than two years, and we have seen them achieve exceptional results. With PointClear, we now help our clients conduct meaningful marketing and sales planning and coordination. This provides directions, objectives and individual plans aligned throughout the organizations to their vision, mission and goals. We have, with PointClear's support, helped clients to bridge the once-impossible gulf between their marketing and sales organizations. Many of our clients have since gone on to produce strong financial results while also building teamwork and cooperation within their organizations.

The end result, in addition to improved financial results, is that our clients are now tracking and measuring the results of their marketing lead-generation and sales efforts to enable senior management to make informed decisions as to what is working, what isn't, and why.

The Truth About Leads is a book with lasting impact. It describes what management must do to improve lead generation and business development. It provides a roadmap of the specific steps to take so that your business can achieve your marketing lead-generation and business-development goals of developing prospects, driving revenue, and consistently producing superior results. It provides the answers to many of your questions about revenues and expenses and marketing and sales working together better than ever before.

In summary, Dan McDade and PointClear know more about lead generation, developing prospects and business development than anyone I know. I proudly recommend this book to you.

Preface: The Truth About Leads

The battle for the success of your company is all about revenue. And it is being lost.

It is being lost on the front line, in the back office and throughout the executive suite. It is being lost early in the sales cycle and at the close.

Every day I talk to companies that are finding that revenue is coming up short, is being left on the table, and can't be sustained. Every day I hear executives complain about numbers not being made, despite much effort and huge investment.

What I notice in these frequent conversations: The organizations that are complaining all have one thing in common. They haven't yet discovered The Truth About Leads—and the role of understanding this truth in the successful quest for revenue.

The Lead: Revered, sought after, valued. At the same time, misunderstood, mishandled, often dismissed. Whether viewed in a lowly or lofty light, the lead is a concept that organizations I converse with have much to learn about, and which is well worth the study.

As I analyze the problem at these organizations, no matter what their size, here is what I find:

- There is no agreement on the definition of a qualified lead.
- Forecasts are thin and/or inaccurate.
- There is no closed loop to measure the effectiveness of marketing programs.
- There is no consensus regarding marketing and sales strategy, including what I call "M$_2$O"—the market, media and offer.

- There are no processes or methodologies to track anything other than the number of leads generated, their cost and total revenue.

Understanding The Truth About Leads is critical—now more than ever—for business-to-business companies like yours. Time is not making the job of generating revenue any easier. It is increasingly difficult to differentiate your company from the pack and acquire new customers. It seems to take massive investments in marketing and sales, people and time to generate even disappointing return. Most of the companies I talk with are finding that what worked five years ago, or even last year, does not necessarily work today. The processes, alignments and initiatives that generated return historically just won't get the job done.

As a consultant, entrepreneur and practitioner of best practices in marketing and sales, I have a front row seat to this struggle: The struggle to keep up, the struggle for the answers, the struggle to find the truth. I have seen the misunderstandings, the misdirected efforts, and the toll they take. I have seen capable and highly motivated executives struggling to answer the same four questions:

- What can I do to earn more revenue?
- How can I increase sales?
- How can I increase market share?
- How can I do more with less?

This book is for C-level executives, vice presidents and directors who seek a framework, processes and the tools to answer these questions. This book is for those who seek The Truth About Leads.

Only when you learn The Truth About Leads, can you:

- Understand the true cost of the gap between marketing and sales.
- Implement a framework that aligns marketing and sales and makes them more productive.

In essence, this book takes you on a journey. Along the path to finding The Truth About Leads, I'll help you identify the critical points where C-level, sales and/or marketing executives take wrong turns as they search for the best practices they know are out there. This book is not about how to plan a marketing campaign, or how to sell. It's about helping you gain a true understanding of that key element of marketing and sales—the lead.

As the owner of a business process outsourcing company, I bring a global perspective to marketing and sales challenges and solutions. Whether the challenge is in front-end business development, markets, media or offers, or back-end components such as sales process development, marketing and/or sales automation or sales management, this book uncovers truths, and in turn provides real solutions based on real work and real successes. When it comes to leads, marketing and sales strategies, operations and tactics, I know what works, what doesn't and why. And, most importantly, I know how to fix what is broken.

By applying the principles and processes explained in this book, you and your company can enjoy the following results:

- Marketing and sales communication and accountability
- Improved marketing and sales productivity
- Additional, larger and more profitable wins
- Accelerated sales cycles
- Enhanced and measurable return on marketing and sales initiatives
- Predictable and more accurate forecasting

- Reductions in marketing and sales costs
- Increased revenue, and a significant edge in this continual battle

I hope you find this book compelling and thought provoking. I invite your comments on both the application of actions suggested herein, as well as the results you attain by following my recommendations.

CHAPTER 1

The Journey: Why I Had to Write a Book About Leads

A significant reason why sales forces don't meet quota has to do with the fact that the word "lead" is so misunderstood. Most companies find other words or phrases to replace it, such as opportunity, qualified sales opportunity, suspect, prospect, pipeline and scores of others. Why? Because leads are misunderstood and as a result, the very word has developed a negative connotation.

Leads are the life blood of any organization; the lack of clarity about what a lead is, how it should be generated, by whom and how it should be worked and tracked is what causes most companies to suffer setbacks or failure. Too, the process of defining, generating, working and tracking leads is a lot more complex than most people think because there are a lot of moving parts and there are a lot of interactions between people that are missed and/or misunderstood.

> Market coverage and lead generation are basic business processes that are broken in most companies. Close to 80 percent of buyers state that when they have been in the market for a solution (such as software or services) they found the vendor, not the other way around.

I once had a client who employed very expensive marketing and sales executives who could not agree on the definition of a lead.

- The chief marketing officer defined leads one way. He was targeting buyers ranging from those in need of a $25,000 point solution all the way up to those with enterprise-level needs.
- The senior vice president of sales defined them another way. He charged his sales team to work $1 million deals only.
- The president of the company, in turn, took a hands-off, just-sell-something approach.

Not only was there not an organization-wide agreement on what the target market was, individual sales executives were not held accountable to follow up marketing leads. These sales reps followed the example of management—they created their own definition of a lead. As it happened, most of the sales executives were elephant hunters and only interested in seven-figure deals—and that's where they applied their time and effort. I remember telling the SVP of sales that he had more sales people than there were seven-figure deals.

Companies that could have benefited from the solutions offered by this client were not contacted by sales, who considered most too small to pursue. In short, marketing generated response, and sales did not follow up.

Not surprisingly, that company failed after spending $100 million (including $250,000 on branding, which was little more than a logo and a color palette). This company's approach to the concept of leads is, sadly, by no means an exception.

Throughout this book, for simplicity and clarity, I am going to use the word "lead" rather than a synonym, and I am going to broadly define what a lead is in this chapter. Other chapters in this book will address more elements of lead definition and the reasons why something that looks so simple is so much more difficult than most people know.

What is a lead? A dictionary definition of a lead follows:

> *Lead: (lēd) n. An individual or company with an actionable need for a service or solution.*

Wikipedia has this to say about leads (in 2010):

> *The identity of a person or entity potentially interested in purchasing a product or service, and represents the first stage of a sales process. Sales leads come from either marketing lead-generation processes such as trade shows, direct marketing, advertising, Internet marketing or from sales person prospecting activities such as cold calling. For a sales lead to qualify as a sales prospect, or equivalently to move a lead from the* **process step sales lead** *to the* **process step sales prospect***, qualification must be performed and evaluated. Typically this involves identifying by direct interrogation the lead's product applicability, availability of funding and time frame for purchase. This is also the entry point of a sales tunnel, sales funnel or sales pipeline.*

Notice the differences in these two definitions. The dictionary states that a lead must have "an actionable need" while Wikipedia states that a lead identifies an "entity potentially interested in purchasing a product or service." Wikipedia goes on to describe more of the process around leads (including, unfortunately, relegating cold calling to the sales force).

Years ago, executives used the acronym MAN (money, authority and need) to define a lead. If there was a budget, if you were talking to a person in a position to make a decision, and if the company had a need for your product or service—you had a lead. Obviously, this terminology is not politically correct and that disfavored acronym was replaced by BANT (budget, authority, need and time frame)—a similar concept, with a time component added. I argue that authority and need are the primary requirements for qualifying a lead (though AN is not nearly as catchy and memorable as BANT). Can a company that does not have a specific time frame and dedicated budget buy based on a business case that is presented to an authority who has pain (also known as "compelling business issue")? Of course! In fact, it happens more than most people think.

In late 1999, I met an extremely intelligent individual who, early in his career, had been accepted into the nuclear submarine program after graduating from the Naval Academy. After leaving the Navy, he took over a successful business that he has since grown dramatically. After he had been working with us for a few months, he said, "Dan, if we could just get clients to close the loop on the leads we generate for them, we will get rich." His point was, we were sending our clients solid gold leads, and those leads were being squandered. Those of us providing the leads, as well as the management of the companies we were providing them for, were banging our heads against the wall as we watched them get discredited, with no follow-up. I remember telling him then, "From your mouth to God's ears," and went on to explain why this understanding was the equivalent of an alchemist finding the formula to inexpensively make gold.

In the decade since then, I am sure that you have read as many articles as I have about ROI, ROMI (return on marketing investment), closing the loop, and aligning marketing and sales. In addition, many of us have spent tens of thousands of dollars (if not hundreds of thousands or millions) on CRM (customer relationship management), SFA (sales force automation) and/or marketing automation solutions designed to track activity and measure return. I argue that lead generation in most companies is a basic business process, one that is broken, and that investments in CRM, SFA and marketing automation have done little or nothing to drive additional revenue.

I had to write a book about leads because I simply could not stand back and watch so much money being wasted. If you are tired of watching your company or companies waste money, the rest of this book is going to tell you what to do about it. This book will tell you The Truth About Leads.

CHAPTER 2

The Gap Between Marketing and Sales Impedes Your Lead Process

One very well-known analyst group documents that 70 percent or more of leads aren't being followed up by sales. Another group claims that 80 percent of marketing investments are wasted. It would be easy to place blame and point fingers. However, neither marketing nor sales executives are really at fault. The responsibility rests with C-level executives and other senior managers who fail to understand or act upon the real problem. The following describes that problem, its cost and some actions you should consider taking to reverse these fatal choices.

Marketing has been rendered powerless in most companies. This function is often seen as one-dimensional, responsible for trade shows, advertising, brochures, websites and in more and more cases, social media. Marketing is given a meager budget and a mandate to generate an impossible number of leads.

The sales force, on the other hand, is frequently filled with people who are misused or wrongly deployed. Companies don't capitalize on their sales people's strengths. Instead, hunters (also called closers) are expected to generate leads and farmers (relationship specialists such as account managers) are expected to close deals. People are being asked to do what they aren't good at—and the results of those requests are inefficiency and ineffectiveness. The responsibility for leveraging the strengths of the team starts at the top.

Marketing has been forced to default to cost-per-lead as the measurement of success for their programs. In keeping with the old expression, "You should never go to war with the sales force," marketing does the best it can to follow senior management's direction and keep its collective head down during inevitable frays. As a result, they're forced to employ methods of lead generation that more often than not produce poor-quality leads.

For too long, marketing has provided sales with no more than low-level leads that are generally a complete waste of time. Unqualified trade show names, unsolicited inquiries, and referrals written on cocktail napkins are often termed leads, and provided to sales. If only five out of 100 leads turned over to sales are actually real opportunities, how much effort do you think your sales force is going to invest in qualifying leads from your company? Not much.

While marketing has contributed its fair share to the lack of good leads, sales is not immune from criticism. Read the scenarios below as examples:

Scenario #1: The following is the background behind a short-term lead once presented to a client. Note the follow-up from the sales representative. Keep in mind that the lead was classified as a short-term opportunity for a company that implements ERP solutions. A 10-minute recording of the conversation, documenting the facts, was provided to the client and, hence, the field sales representative:

"ABC Company is a division of [well-known parent company]. ABC Company is a contractor for the Department of Defense. The company plans to replace its ERP system. [Prospect's First Name] wants a more versatile ERP system that will handle manufacturing processes throughout the organization. The company is currently using a [Legacy Solution] it has had in place for the past eight years. The company has not begun to evaluate solutions, but its initial intention is to select a solution like PeopleSoft® or Oracle®. A steering committee and analysis committee will be in place to evaluate a potential solution. A

budget has not been determined, although the purchase is expected to be a capital item during the next fiscal year [approximately three months away]. [Our client] should make contact immediately and stay in touch to keep advised."

The prospect went on to describe problems with a proprietary database, a budget estimate of approximately $400,000 and an openness to communicate immediately with our client.

What was the sales representative's response? "Not a lead. No reason for follow-up." Without even a single discussion, this individual decided that his company didn't have an opportunity in this large manufacturing company (which, by the way, was in the sweet spot of their target market). The reason? "Decision-making time frame too far out."

The sales representative, no doubt, read that it might take longer than one quarter for this deal to close. Like many sales representatives who survive on a quarter-to-quarter basis, it was apparently too onerous to consider either attempting to accelerate the process and decision-making time frame and/or nurturing the account to write, rather than respond to, the RFP when it was issued. As one might expect, the prospect was compelled (by a competitor) to begin the investigation sooner rather than later and our client was not even in the hunt, much less short-listed, when it could have owned the evaluation. A smarter, and/or better managed, sales representative won the business for a competitor.

Scenario #2: I recently discovered that a short-term lead presented to a client a year ago was barely followed up by sales. That prospect recently inked a seven-figure deal with a competitor of our client. When I asked the client to research what happened, it was discovered that the sales representative had spent several thousand dollars creating and binding white papers for a presentation to the prospect, sent the bound documents to the prospect, and then never called to follow up.

Scenario #3: On behalf of a large company that sells a technology product to colleges and universities, my organization contacted just over 100 schools in July—the peak buying season. More than 40 of the schools had not heard from their sales rep for "some time," even though the company dedicates sales reps to this market. The school-to-rep coverage model was very manageable. The bottom line: The sales representatives were not getting the job done. So while the giant slept, competitors were gaining market share. Incredibly, the same sales force killed a program focused on following up with another portion of the same market to make sure that a back-to-school campaign was being properly executed. The reason? Sales representatives were "too busy to help" identify target contacts and really did not want someone in their accounts at that time. It would be laughable if it were not so costly.

As hard as it is to admit, the same stories—or worse—could be told about your company. If you find that leads are not closing, begin the process of finding out why!

Remember the following statistics for all qualified leads:

- Ten percent will close within three months.
- Another 16 percent will close within six months.
- Another 19 percent will close in one year.

A total of 45 percent of qualified leads end up buying from your company or a competitor within a year. How effective is your company at staying on top of qualified leads?

The battle is raging between marketing and sales, but when the smoke clears, it is companies that are getting hurt. You must define the process that will lead to success. Until you do, your company will stagnate, or worse.

Here is what to do:

A Five-step Program to Close the Gap

1. *Stop the carousel on marketing programs.* The tendency is to be afraid of jeopardizing short-term sales by doing anything different. But take a look at all of your planned programs—advertising, trade show promotions, direct marketing, webinars—and stop or cut back the ones you can while you take the time to evaluate their effectiveness. Don't keep the merry-go-round going just because they're already started. Stop, recalibrate and make sure these programs are moving in the right direction.

2. *Plan to crawl, walk and run.* You will not be able to roll out tested marketing programs next month. No company can effectively impact current quarter results with current quarter marketing. Don't try. Instead, plan carefully and execute thoughtfully for long-term sales success.

3. *Pinpoint your market.* For example, one client used a market research firm that determined that the prospect universe exceeded 80,000 companies. Almost immediately we cut the universe in half by focusing on larger opportunities that closed as easily as smaller opportunities and represented profitable business rather than marginal business. After another six months or so, we reduced the prospect universe to just under 30,000 companies based on back-end analyses that included close rates by vertical. Currently, that client targets approximately 22,000 companies and we will, no doubt, continue to work the universe down based on the appropriateness of the fit and the potential margin to our client. NOTE: I don't recommend depending on one list source to build your database. The best databases contain data from multiple sources which are then verified and enhanced five to 10 percent at a time.

4. *Test your market, media and offer before investing.* Before spending significant dollars on a marketing program, it is imperative that you test your list or database (market), the communication platforms you plan to use (media), and your price, package, terms, guarantee, differentiators, etc. (offer). Simple as this seems, it almost never happens. This practical testing step can hugely impact sales and save tens of thousands of dollars.

5. *Measure your results.* If you do not have a process to track and measure the ROI of your marketing programs, you are just throwing darts. Only by quantifying the success of each program can you know if your efforts are worthwhile. In fact, you may be surprised to find that anecdotal evidence does not align with the facts. Here's an example: One of my clients complained that the company's cost-per-lead was too high. While I don't advocate measuring cost-per-lead, as quality is far more important, we proceeded to examine this situation. When we took a close look—by breaking out the costs—we learned that the cost-per-lead generated through trade show programs was indeed too high, as were those generated through response management programs. These leads were costing $1,500 and $1,000 each, respectively. Leads generated through pure cold calling, on the other hand, were running $500 each. It's important to note that lead quality across the programs was consistent. This kind of analysis gives you the power to make the right decisions concerning your marketing programs.

CHAPTER 3

Why Your Sales Force Needs Fewer Leads

Yes, you read the title correctly. Sales reps don't need more leads. They need fewer leads—or more accurately, fewer raw, unfiltered, unqualified leads.

Good sales reps are by nature hunters, eager to close in for the kill. Take Steve, for example. Watch what happens when he receives a stack of leads: He rifles through them seeking the ideal prospect.

- Not a senior executive? Out.
- Budget undefined? Goodbye.
- Next-year decision? No way.

Steve is obviously making some poor decisions. For example, a recent study found that for technology products and services, line-of-business managers and functional titles are much better lead sources than senior executives. And the average technology purchase starts as an inquiry on the Internet and can often take a year or more until fruition.

But to be fair to Steve, he is paid to sell—not to interpret leads. Moreover, he is jaded from bad marketing practices. In his rookie year, he wasted enormous amounts of time following up on so-called A+ leads from marketing. As it turned out, one-fourth had erroneous phone numbers and addresses. Another 20 percent came from consultants, competitors and students. Most of the others had little or no pre-qualification information. None had been filtered or nurtured in any way by marketing. ("That's not our role," said the marketing manager.)

More Leads Doesn't Equal More Success

Meanwhile, in the marketing department, Jennifer is completing her monthly report.

"We're on track for a great quarter in lead generation," she writes. *"This month we generated 1,278 leads from all sources—that's a 30 percent gain over last year! And in spite of higher ad rates, we continue to keep our cost-per-lead under $100!"*

Jennifer's report says nothing about lead qualification, how leads are nurtured, or what the sales force has done with previous leads. This leaves one to wonder: Does anyone in this company's management understand why investments in sales and marketing are not resulting in closed business? Do they realize that the real money spent to create leads is wasted unless they are managed and monitored to ensure a return?

The true measure of successful marketing should be how well marketing creates sales opportunities that have a high potential of developing into sales. The true measure of sales should be how well they close these good leads from marketing.

Far too many companies, however, evaluate marketing's success by the number of leads they hand to sales. These companies do not have effective processes and methodologies to track anything other than the number of leads generated and their cost. Many of the same companies fail to hold sales accountable for closing the good leads and for reporting back results that feed the marketing and sales model. The overall result is often wasted marketing dollars and wasted sales time.

Closing the Gap Between Marketing and Sales

How can the blame game between sales and marketing be resolved? What if, instead of reporting how many low-value leads marketing sent to Steve and his colleagues, Jennifer reported the following:

"This month, marketing added 14 new prospects to our Prospect Development program. A total of 41 sales opportunities are currently under development by marketing.

"In June, sales received 10 fully nurtured sales opportunities representing $3.5 million in potential near-term revenue. I have attached a summary report."

PROSPECT DEVELOPMENT REPORT							
Sales rep	**Company & decision maker**	**Revenue potential**	**First contact date**	**# of weeks lead nurtured**	**# of program touch points**	**Hand-off to rep date**	**Decision "expected by" date**
Barrett	Pine Mtn (CFO)	550k	4/21	7	8	6/10	Oct
	Westland Co (COO)	825k	4/17	8	8	6/14	Nov
Floyd	FlexFast Mfg (Committee)	280k	4/3	12	8	6/28	Dec
	Sanders Inc (Exec VP)	180k	5/17	4	11	6/16	Dec
Jones	HMS Inc (COO)	400k	4/25	6	9	6/6	Oct
	Collins Co (Project Ldr)	120k	3/28	12	14	6/20	Nov

As indicated by the highlighted rows in Jennifer's Prospect Development report (see above), sales representative Carol Barrett received two qualified leads this month. Each had already been contacted at least eight times; the best touchpoint techniques use multiple media—some combination of phone, voice message and email. Each lead is deemed to have graduated from unknown or long-term status to a near-term decision-making mode. For each developed lead, marketing provided Carol a complete contact history, a company profile, and a thorough overview of the budget, the decision timeline, individuals involved in the decision, any events or other factors driving the decision, pain points, hot buttons and competition.

When presented with a few well-qualified leads, Carol gives them priority attention. For one thing, she knows her regional manager will be inquiring about them. More importantly, she knows from experience that these leads are real or she would not be getting them. Her company has already established a relationship with the decision maker, who is expecting Carol's call.

Which lead-generation machine would your company's sales force prefer—the one that gives Steve reams of unfiltered leads, or the one that gives Carol two sales opportunities expected to close within six months?

CHAPTER 4

Reaping the Value of Long-Term Leads

In 1885, William Lever of Lever Bros. said, "Half of the marketing money you spend is wasted—trouble is you don't know which half." Unfortunately, there is a good chance that substantially more than half of your marketing investments are being squandered.

Many leads are not followed up by sales, for legitimate *and* non-intuitive reasons. The legitimate reasons for no follow-up are that the leads are obviously low-end and unfiltered. They may be companies from the wrong verticals, too small to be in the market, or they may be students/consultants who responded to an offer. Non-intuitive reasons include the "I called three times and didn't get a call back." Basically, if the lead is hard to work, it is often dismissed. As few as five percent of leads are followed up by sales.

- Long-term leads are mostly ignored by sales as they are not seen as helpful in impacting the current period's quota.
- Companies that are qualified without immediate interest are ignored by sales and marketing—a huge waste as the expense to identify those that are qualified versus those that are not is often duplicated and the potential benefit lost.

It has always been my contention that time frame on leads should be virtually ignored and that long-term leads are actually more valuable than short-term leads. Let's review some important considerations about both short- and long-term leads:

- About one-third of short-term leads are actually hot leads. In many cases, these hot lead opportunities are already baked, meaning that these buying companies have already been sold by another vendor. They seem hot initially because they have indicated that they have a short buying cycle, and they are eager to talk. But what these buyers are likely doing is validating a decision already made, or looking to you for what is frequently called column fodder—price comparison after the fact to justify an already-chosen vendor. If your company fairs well late in an evaluation, hot leads can be valuable. However, due to the nature of entering an evaluation late, it's always wise to carefully pick your battles when it comes to investing cycles in hot leads.
- Short-term leads that are not hot are actually better. These are defined as leads that are within a one or two sales cycle time frame of closing. They require immediate attention, are not working under an RFI or an RFP, and no decision has yet been made.
- Long-term leads provide the opportunity to define, if not manage, the buying process. With these opportunities, the worst case is that you have a great chance at being short-listed, and in the best case you are invited to design the RFP and bake the process in favor of your company and against a late entrant.

Take a look at the models represented in the following tables for an example of the value of best practices in handling short- and long-term leads:

ROI WITHOUT Best-Practice Handling of Short- and Long-Term Leads			
Category	Quantity Short Term	Quantity Long Term	Total
Names	1,000	N/A	
Short-term leads	30		
Long-term leads		N/A	
% Closed ST leads	20%		
% Closed LT leads		N/A	
# of deals	6		
Average deal	$250,000	N/A	
Revenue	$1,500,000		
Cost of qualification	$59,040		
Gross after marketing expense	$1,440,960	N/A	$1,440,960

ROI WITH Best-Practice Handling of Short- and Long-Term Leads			
Category	Quantity Short Term	Quantity Long Term	Total
Names	1,000		
Short-term leads	40		
Long-term leads		40	
% Closed ST leads	20%		
% Closed LT leads		20%	
# of deals	8	8	
Average deal	$250,000	$250,000	
Revenue	$2,000,000	$2,000,000	
Cost of qualification	$59,040	$4,920	
Gross after marketing expense	$1,940,960	$1,995,080	$3,936,040

1) Our experience is that inside sales resources (within companies) and their sales forces miss opportunities due to either lack of market identification and/or lack of lead follow-through.
2) Once filtered, the percentage of long-term leads that close should actually be higher.
3) Note the efficiency of nurturing longer-term leads on an incremental cost basis before being turned over to sales (two cycles of contact).

Sales were comparatively easy to find during the salad days of the late '90s and to some extent even in the mid-2000s. One client I work with kidded that just a few years ago any sales representative who responded to an RFP made plan, and they made club if they spell-checked the response. Since then, the following changes have occurred:

- The market has moved from a buying model based on vision creation—an idealistic approach that works with unjaded prospects—to one requiring proof and value.
- Short-term lead rates have held while long-term leads have dropped dramatically.
- No Decision outcomes have increased dramatically.

In many cases there is not much a sales executive can do about a sales process that ends in No Decision by the target company. The fact that there are more of them today is explained by the following:

- A shift away from user-oriented approval processes to higher level and more committee-oriented decision-making.
- Disenchantment with ROI on past purchases.
- Battening down of the hatches in the face of an up-and-down economy.

In light of these changes, it's more important than ever that smart companies ensure follow-up on every lead, and infuse within the company the value of long-term leads. Capitalizing on long-term leads is probably the best way to secure the future of your organization, not to mention to reap more return on marketing investment. Short-sighted companies will not fare well; those with aggressive sales and marketing approaches will.

The Proof Is In the Numbers

Most managers would gladly spend $4,920 to generate $1,995,080 in incremental revenue ($3,936,040 minus the $1,940,960). Here are some reasons why this perfectly logical idea is so infrequently executed, much less well executed:

- The sales force is driven by quarterly results (often due to the fact that public companies live and die by those numbers). As a result, even the best-intentioned sales executives cannot afford to focus on long-term leads as they search, often without success, for shorter-term opportunities.

- Marketing is faulted for generating both too few leads, and leads that are not of high quality. Yet, marketing infrequently receives feedback on individual leads. Often marketing hears nothing at all, or general feedback that "the leads were no good." As a result, a frustrated management creates a numeric metric—measuring marketing's success based on the number of leads generated, or the cost-per-lead. Given this collision of circumstances—little detailed feedback on leads, and incentives based on quantity and cost—marketing ends up being driven to buy the greatest number of leads for the lowest price possible, rationalizing that "sales is probably just going to complain anyway" and "I have been told by management to drive the cost-per-lead down."

- There is no process or method to close the loop on leads in most companies. Even sophisticated SFA and CRM solutions are only as good as the data that is input into them. Frequently, information input by sales is limited due to other priorities, the pressure to produce results AND, most importantly, the visibility and overhead associated with everyone having access to prospect information. This results in endless questions from direct

31

and indirect managers and unwanted accountability on the part of the sales executive.

Here is what I recommend:

- CAREFULLY define a qualified lead. No matter how tight you think the definition is, you will be surprised if you ask every marketing and sales executive what their definition is. You will get a different answer from each of them.
- Make sure that your market is targeted. Most companies' prospect lists are so broad that a lot of money is wasted marketing to non-prospects.
- Measure the cost of short- and long-term leads. And measure the value.
- Make sure that front-end costs (cost-per-lead), as well as back-end costs (cost-per-closed-sale), are measured. If you are not doing this, figure out what it is going to take to do it and start now.
- If you value your current lead-generation efforts, put all short-term leads on the forecast at 10 percent using your average deal size. Require a sales management executive's approval to remove one of these leads from the forecast. Use this process to both measure the quality of the leads generated and measure the effectiveness of your sales force in following up on leads. Lead audits, or what we call Prospect Satisfaction Analyses, are incredibly powerful and accomplish both needs.
- If you do not value your current lead-generation efforts, do something about it and then follow the steps above.

If you are ignoring your long-term leads, you are wasting significant dollars, energy and other resources. Systematic nurturing of long-term opportunities is your best strategy for effectively increasing your marketing and sales program, and succeeding for the long haul.

Lead Nurturing: Who's Minding the Lead Farm?

Research shows that 45 percent of qualified leads will end up buying a solution from someone within a year.

Think of lead qualification as a funnel. Marketing pours raw, unfiltered leads from a variety of sources into the top of the funnel. Ideally, what emerges at the other end—ready for professional handling by a lead-hungry sales force—is a steady supply of qualified opportunities, each with a defined process and time frame for buying.

Reality, unfortunately, rarely matches the ideal. All too often, no one is managing what happens to leads once they enter the funnel. Marketing, by focusing on lead cost instead of quality, thinks it has done its job simply by dumping in the unfiltered leads. No one contacts or qualifies the inquirers. No one augments the leads with demographic and firmographic data. No one nurtures long-term suspects into short-term prospects. No one evaluates the effectiveness of the lead sources.

In this garbage-in, garbage-out scenario, you can't blame sales representatives for ignoring the output. Who, then, should process leads?

Since only a small portion of freshly generated leads typically fall into the short-term category, the root of the broken lead-generation system is that little or no effort is being made to determine whether each raw lead has any potential at all, much less whether it is short-term or long-term.

Whose job is lead filtration, qualification and development? In my observation of how hundreds of companies treat leads, the bulk of the work overwhelmingly rests with sales—and that is a recipe for failure. Even if leads are pre-qualified, salespeople are notoriously poor at following up on any leads but the hottest. In fact, experts say that sales does not follow up more than 70 percent of leads provided to them.

Management rightfully motivates and compensates salespeople to focus on making the immediate numbers, not on building a pipeline of prospects. To fully leverage the talents of your sales force, don't expect sales representatives to filter leads, qualify them, and then cultivate the long-term ones until they are qualified sales opportunities. They just won't do it!

Traditional marketing departments are also not the best equipped for this important job. They are filled with brand builders or communicators who do not possess lead-management skills and technology, and/or they are being measured on response rates and cost-per-lead, which are the wrong metrics.

In my experience, best practices suggest that a separate group, inside or outside the company, needs to take control of the vital lead-development function. Think of this group of specialists as lead farmers—they qualify raw leads, nurture lukewarm prospects into the hot category, and turn the developed leads over to the sales force for harvesting. Often this process takes months.

A developed lead is one that sets the stage for relationship selling. A lead farmer equips the sales representative with in-depth knowledge about the prospect. With advance insight into the prospect's motivations, pain points and buying plans, the sales rep can engage the prospect in a consultative conversation rather than launching into a cold-call presentation or a discovery interview.

There has always been a lot of confusion around lead nurturing. It is sometimes called drip marketing and it can also be confused with closed-loop marketing. Recently, many companies have come to view marketing automation solutions as the holy grail of lead management and nurturing—thinking, incorrectly, that these systems are so powerful you can theoretically automate the prospect experience from web visit to sales hand-off.

The fact that not every person wants to be treated like the human equivalent of a pinball—receiving personal attention only after hitting the right bumpers and scoring the right points—is a major problem for companies that overly depend on marketing automation. Without appropriate intervention a tremendous amount of opportunity is lost (the vendors offering these exciting solutions are the first to agree).

I will provide a sample lead-nurturing schedule, but first want to talk about the numbers behind lead generation and nurturing and how the first three cycles of lead generation work prior to moving toward lead-nurturing cycles.

I'll start with the numbers:

What a Sample Targeted Direct Marketing Campaign Looks Like

ABC Company retains a firm to execute a call-email-call program against a targeted list of accounts with the results expected being opportunities for sales follow-up. Let's assume for the moment that the list is targeted, the definition of a lead has been agreed upon and the vendor executing the program has qualified people to effectively run the campaign. (In my experience, this is a generous scenario, and not realistic.)

The following are the results after the first time through the list of companies:

Results (1,000 targets)	
Opportunities	50
Qualified Companies With No Immediate Interest	350
Not Qualified Companies	300
Unknown (did not reach, no response to multi-touch after one cycle)	300

Using best practices (telephone, email, mail) the results would spur the following activities:

- Delivery of opportunities to the field as uncovered. Monitor field follow-up. If any opportunity becomes inactive (sales rep can't connect with prospect), return it immediately for reheating.

- Begin the second cycle of multi-touch, multi-media, multi-cycle campaign against the 350 companies that are qualified with no immediate interest. The first touch of the new (second) cycle should be personalized based on research about the company and the individual or individuals targeted and follow-up on any trigger events (change of management, acquisition or disposition of a company, etc.). This is an opportunity to send a hand-written note attached to an article pertinent to your prospect or, better yet, a success story about one of your clients in the same industry as your prospect.

- Test 10 percent of the Not Qualified Companies after carefully segmenting them by SIC or NAICS and size and verify that they are, in fact, not qualified. I find that this is a good test and that you frequently find nuggets of gold in this group.

- For the fourth result set, begin the second cycle as stated above—treat this group as Qualified with No Immediate Interest until you know otherwise.

Every market is different and higher-level decision makers require more touches than do lower-level decision makers. However, the following is an example of the first cycle—a three-touch program for a group of 50 targeted prospects (note that the total number of companies being worked at any given point is about 100):

Sample Lead-Nurturing Schedule – Cycle One	
Week One	Up to five navigation dials, one voicemail and one email
Week Two	Up to five more attempts, two voicemails and two emails
Week Three	Two attempts and one direct mail package (sent overnight)
Week Six	Repeat Week One (navigation dials are converted into additional attempts)
Week Seven	Repeat Week Two
Week Eight	Repeat Week Three
Week Eleven	Repeat Week Six
Week Twelve	Repeat Week Two
Week Thirteen	Repeat Week Three

Please note that voicemails and emails build on and complement one another. Additional attempts during weeks two, six, seven, 11 and 12 should be made at different times of the day, including break and lunch times.

Over the course of a quarter, you will have invested approximately 36 attempts, left nine voicemails and sent nine emails for a total of 54 touches. A lot of people ask me if that is too many touches. They ask if we don't frequently get calls from these targets saying, "Stop calling me!" In truth, professionally developed programs rarely result in that feedback. In fact, the CFO of one of the country's top five utilities actually called one of my team members back at the 42nd touch to tell us to keep calling. "You are my conscience and I need to be reminded. I am busy now but intend to get to this issue soon. Please keep calling." Eventually this opportunity turned into a $1 billion deal for my client.

You don't, of course, simply repeat this process quarter after quarter without change. As you learn more about each company the cycle may accelerate—or decelerate based on prospect-specific issues. Companies merge or close—and then you have to start over with fresh new prospects. I find it effective to invest up to three full cycles (such as the one described in this chapter), varying the message and being more and more specific to the prospect as more is learned about their business.

I have seen cycles like the one described above go on for three years before the prospect finally converts to a lead that closed for my client.

Fewer than 20 percent of companies have effective lead-nurturing programs. If you are

Qualified Prospects

More Buyers

Raw Leads

Few Buyers

Too many raw, unqualified leads can create a clogged marketing and sales process and an unhealthy sales funnel.

not using the CRM or SFA (or even just a spreadsheet) to capture touch information and track results—you are wasting a lot of money and missing a lot of opportunity.

CHAPTER 5

Turning Raw Leads Into Real Opportunities – Don't Give Up Too Soon!

Lead farmers—those charged with nurturing leads until they're ready to buy—have a challenging job. The starting point is usually an inquiry consisting of a name, title, company and phone number or email address. The lead farmer must have the patience, discipline and skill to engage the inquirer in a conversation. This step alone can take weeks or months.

Many of the best prospects turn out to be those who have been contacted multiple times by voicemail, email and direct mail over a period of months before a conversation finally occurs. Executives often don't respond until a need's priority has escalated.

The lesson: Don't give up too early. Many executives save emails and even voicemails, and will eventually self-qualify by responding or replying at a time convenient for them and after they have satisfied themselves with independent research and have come to the conclusion that your solution or service is a fit. You may get a response to a letter or email sent weeks or months or even years ago, or shorter-term prospects might respond when the latest touch-point coincides with the prospect's need window.

After a dialog has been opened, the lead farmer begins probing, documenting and tracking—always with the aim of moving the lead further through the pipeline. The lead farmer is patient, but persistent. He or she is also creative and informative.

If he or she is perceived as selling too hard, the potential buyer may be put off. If an otherwise well-qualified prospect is stalled due to budgeting or other considerations, the lead farmer follows up meticulously at the appropriate time. Ultimately, the lead farming specialist will either disqualify the lead if nothing happens, or turn over a fully developed short-term lead to sales.

Attributes of a Well-Qualified Lead

A qualified, short-term lead typically has 10 attributes (see box at right). Unfiltered leads rarely have more than three of these attributes, so any sales rep working on a commission check will be delighted to get all 10. With a detailed picture of the prospect's business drivers, plans and buying processes, the sales rep is positioned as a knowledgeable advisor interested in the prospect's business challenges.

Clearly, the lead farming role is incompatible with the sales role. Good lead farmers are hard to find. The best approach to performing the job effectively is to (A) assign it to a specialized in-house team with no direct sales responsibility, or (B) outsource it to a firm totally focused on nurturing leads into sales opportunities. But whatever you do, don't give unfiltered, unqualified leads to your sales team.

> **ATTRIBUTES OF A WELL-QUALIFIED LEAD**
>
> 1. SIC or NAICS Code.
> 2. Firmographics (revenue, # of employees, # of locations).
> 3. Decision makers and influencers identified.
> 4. Environment documented.
> 5. Decision maker engaged.
> 6. Business pain(s) uncovered/validated.
> 7. Decision-making process and time frame documented.
> 8. Budget allocated or process for budgeting documented.
> 9. Competitive landscape documented.
> 10. Sense of urgency or compelling event exists.

CHAPTER 6

What Works: Introduction to Market, Media and Offer (M$_2$O)

Ah, Saturday. An early game of tennis, some family time, maybe a power nap with the fragrant promise of the choice T-bone you've been waiting to grill tempting you onward through the day. The sun starts to sink; you saunter out to pre-heat the gas grill to searing readiness. Turning the knob, you get...nothing. The bolt specially designed to control the gas line has vanished.

You vaguely recall tossing the extra one provided by the manufacturer into an overflowing box of miscellaneous fasteners you keep in the basement. Unearthing it, you are faced with at least 158 shiny, seemingly identical bolts—but only one will work. It's getting dark, you're getting hungry, and the longed-for explosion of chargrilled beef taste is slipping further away, buried in 157 indistinguishable bits of metal that aren't quite right.

Now you know how your sales team feels.

The very best of them are unwaveringly focused on the end result. They visualize that steak, they hunger to sink their teeth into as big a bite as they possibly can, they know just how high the heat should be, just when to grab the meat off the grate and slap it down on the plate, sizzling and perfect. If you give them one bolt, or even three or four, they'll test them and turn them, find the one that works, hook up that gas and turn up the flames. If you give them 158, they'll throw out the box and start looking around for another way to cook.

This is exactly what happens with typical lead generation. About 95 percent of generated leads are not effectively pursued by sales. Sales organizations eager to close deals are frustrated by the very thing that marketers are rewarded for: a mountain of leads. Rather than sort through a motley group of prospects—some not qualified, others not sales ready—they abandon all but the most obvious and substitute those leads with their own, usually less successful, prospecting.

With companies increasingly forced to do more with fewer resources, figuring out which leads will cut to the chase fastest becomes someone else's problem. Marketing has done its job in initiating interest and sales converts the most interested to revenue. But who takes the existing market curiosity, sharpens it by exposing underlying pressure points, whets interest with repeated contact and files away the unqualified prospects, pointing sales toward only the most potent opportunities? An agreement on the importance of these functions—and who's responsible—is absolutely necessary.

My clients find that a prospect pool enticed by marketing and honed by a specific process delivers leads that need their product, fit qualifying parameters, are favorably pre-disposed to their brand and are ready to be sold. The sales teams, armed with precise business information on the prospects' pains and priorities, are ready to sell.

That specific process referred to above is facilitated by a discipline called M_2O. M_2O helps pinpoint the best prospects, build familiarity with their organizations and their needs, and use that intelligence to craft messaging that directly targets the state of readiness. Those simple, sound practices often get lost between a large-scale marketing campaign and the immediate pressure to close, but they are keys to reaping the most revenue from both. M_2O—Market, Media and Offer—is examined in detail in the following three sections.

Market – Why Direct Marketing Causes Executives to Lose Their Marbles

The first "M" in M₂O focuses on tightly defining your market by:

- Industry
- Geography
- Firmographics
- Titles
- Psychographics

Many marketers, reluctant to miss any avenue of opportunity, define their market as broadly as possible and, in doing so, miss the chance to convincingly address the most potent prospects. A typical example is a company that perceives its target market to be the Fortune 1000. That group is actually comprised of several thousand revenue reporting companies—some with centralized and some with decentralized decision making. This market definition is simply not meaningful, and will cause confusion and inefficiency among the marketing and sales teams.

While it sounds contradictory, I recommend that companies identify the largest but most targeted markets possible to make sure that they have a tightly defined universe. Only once the market has been carefully defined can contacts be identified and contact information around those targets built that form the foundation for multi-touch, multi-media, multi-cycle prospect development programs. (This approach to program implementation is covered in detail later in this book.)

Once the market has been defined, the next step is to segment it. Companies that more quickly see the value proposition of a vendor's product, whether due to immediate business pains or because they are looking to enhance their own capabilities, respond at higher levels than others. So it makes sense to identify segments of the market that are more likely to buy, and market to them specifically.

Others, though still qualified, may be more hesitant and require different touch strategies and messaging before their sales potential can mature. They are still good sources of revenue though, and if left behind in the rush to close more near-term business will most likely end up ceding revenue to a more patient competitor. Recognizing and nurturing all prospect potential is crucial to pipeline development, future revenue and market share.

By applying market intelligence and finely defined segmentation strategies, I have been successful in increasing sales performance while actually reducing marketing costs.

List Basics

The most misunderstood aspects of "market" as pertaining to direct marketing involve lists and databases. Executives often feel that lists are a waste of their time, and database issues seem so complex that they are willing to pay exorbitant sums to the "experts" who deal with them. Big mistake!

Over 60 percent of the value of any direct marketing campaign is driven by list and database issues. For most business-to-business marketers there are a number of list choices: response lists, subscriber lists, controlled circulation publications, compiled files, etc. They each have advantages and disadvantages, but it is important to know that even the best lists are rarely more than 50 percent accurate.

To understand why, think about marbles. Ever play marbles? Remember that different types of marbles had different values:

Marble Price List	
Swirls	$0.25
Stripes	$1.25
Flecks	$1.25
Loops	$1.25
Spirals	$1.25
Agates	$5.00

What if I told you that your direct marketing campaigns are run as though you were playing marbles without knowing the difference between a Swirl and an Agate? Worse, what if improving results was as simple as separating your Swirls from your Agates?

While most executives would not dream of buying a jar of marbles without knowing exactly what was inside, they approve the purchase of lists that contain the equivalent of Swirls, Flecks and Agates, often without knowing exactly what they are getting.

Suppose you have a mason jar filled with the following:

100 Swirls – $25
100 Flecks – $125
100 Agates – $500

The average value of each marble in the jar is $2.17. Reach in and grab an Agate for $2.17 and you have cause for celebration. Pay $2.17 for a Swirl and you will feel taken.

When you execute a direct marketing program you make essentially the same choice. You mail, call or otherwise contact individuals based on their potential value to you as a customer. Some names are worth very little (let's compare these names to Swirls at $0.25), some are average in value (say, the value of a Fleck at $1.25) and some are high-value names (such as an Agate for $5.00).

Is it possible to market to just the high-value names? Yes! It is possible to market to the Agates and Flecks, and skip the Swirls in your market with just a little effort and very little expense.

Here is how:

Simple Market Segmentation

Just as you can see the difference between a Swirl and an Agate when you look into the jar of marbles, it is possible to calculate the value of names you direct market to in advance by doing a bit of testing prior to rolling out campaigns.

The secret is segmentation. Segmentation breaks large universes of names (multiple lists and/or multiple list segments) into smaller, homogeneous "cubes" or layers of like individuals or companies. Once these cubes are identified, response from each can be separately analyzed. Some differentiating characteristics to use when segmenting names into cubes are geography, revenue, number of employees, growth percentages, SIC codes, decision-making levels and/or other data that is commonly available. You should also compare each list or list segment to your customer list and those of your competitors to determine how many customers match your prospect lists. The higher the match you find, the better the list.

If you pay $5 for a marble you expect to own an Agate. Think of lists the same way. Find the Agates, and touch more of them than you do Swirls, and you will enjoy a higher ROI every time. With segmentation, a list is split into distinct strata of names "cubed" by similarities rather than a random "jar of marbles." Just picture your Swirls, Flecks and Agates all segmented by type and you have the right picture.

The following is a deeper dive into this subject—the objective is to help you win all the marbles (without losing yours).

A Deeper Dive Into Relational Segmentation
(For Those Who Want More Detail On This Subject)

People around me for any length of time have heard me say (probably multiple times) that there is no such thing as a good list. Each company is different and every market is different. At one time I had three very large ERP companies as clients and despite the fact that they sold to seemingly like companies, each of their markets was different in some way.

There are two issues that most companies deal with regarding lists or databases:

- Wasting dollars, resources and time trying to clean up outdated, in-house databases to generate profitable leads at a reasonable cost; or
- Sourcing lists from unscrupulous list brokers and managers who sell out of a black box and whose lists yield poor results.

Cleaning up in-house databases and prospecting into new markets is not impossible, but often these black holes have become final resting places for hundreds, and even thousands, of records characterized by sparse, inaccurate information. These so-called databases have provided little value to the company that owns or has bought them.

Is there an efficient, cost-effective way to run cleanup and marketing initiatives that will generate higher returns? You bet!

Sophisticated technology and processes can help you wisely test your customer and prospect databases and establish predictors of success before you deploy broad-based cleanup and lead-generation initiatives.

The strategic approach I recommend provides companies with the market intelligence they need to fully fund and roll out programs targeted to high-return segments. This model has increased individual campaign results by up to 50 percent and simultaneously decreased costs by as much as 35 percent.

Traditional Cleanups Miss Potential

The mandate to clean up and use in-house databases is grounded in a rock-solid objective: Leverage existing customer and prospect data to drive cross-selling, up-selling and new sales. Easier said than done, however, as companies often struggle with many disparate customer, prospect and partner databases. These databases are often characterized by outdated, inaccurate or sparse information about customers in four critical areas:

- Current pains and visions for addressing them.
- Current technology environment.
- Correct decision-making team and buying process.
- Plans for short- or mid-term purchases.

Still, your gut tells you there is opportunity hidden in these databases. The question is, "How can we best clean them and mine them for value?" Conventional wisdom calls for running a Phase I database cleanup initiative followed by a Phase II lead-generation program, setting in motion a one-two punch with high expectations. Yes, the data will be a little better, and some leads will shake out. A few deals may even close.

But, all too often, return falls far short of potential. Campaigns that should do well don't, and time, resources and dollars are wasted. Why? Traditional cleanup programs only focus on replacing dirty or absent data with fresh, correct data. They do not add the segmentation or prioritization value needed to predict success. As a result, marketing campaigns can only target all cleaned names, because the best names have not been identified.

Head-to-Head Comparison

ABC Software's three in-house databases help contrast traditional database cleanup/marketing with a different, more strategic approach. The table below describes a license customer database, a maintenance customer database, and a prospect list purchased from a technology list vendor.

ABC Software Databases	
List Code	**List Description**
C1	Customer List 1 • Software licenses only
C2	Customer List 2 • Maintenance and contract licenses
P1	Prospect List 1 • Purchased list for telemarketing • Example: Compiled list • Names match targeted vertical, revenue and geography criteria

ABC Software knows there are many opportunities for new sales, up-sells, cross-sells, and point sales in its databases. It has the following objectives for Phase I database cleanup:

- Call and update firmographic data for companies in the databases.
- Verify decision makers and contact information.

...along with these objectives for Phase II database marketing:

- Identify current addressable pain and projects.
- Segment the results by opportunity, time frame and budget.
- Distribute the hottest opportunities to field sales.

Strategic Targeting Approach Needed

Using a traditional database cleanup and database marketing approach, ABC Software cleans up one list at a time and runs a lead-generation program into each. Predictably, less than ideal outcomes occur.

> A traditional database marketing program targets all cleaned names in the database, when only a fraction of the names warrant investment.

While the cleaned database now has updated contact information, the lack of a strategic targeting approach means the cleanup has added no segmentation or prioritization value to the records. The large investment of dollars and resources has failed to provide high-return direction or projected potential for Phase II database marketing. This assumes, of course, the cleanup initiative hasn't broken the budget and left nothing for a Phase II marketing initiative.

Without the intelligence needed to hierarchically rank the valuable records that deserve to be contacted, a traditional database marketing program targets all cleaned names in the database, when only a fraction of the names warrant investment.

There may be limited success with lead generation, as shown in the table on the next page.

Response Rates From Traditional Phase II Database Marketing	
Source Database or List	**Lead Rate by Source**
C1 – License-only base	5%
C2 – Maintenance base	7%
P1 – Prospect list	3%

But return will never match potential because there is no deployment of dollars and resources against segments known or predicted to generate best return. No one knows why small successes were achieved or what portions of the list generated above or below average returns. Without benchmarks, there are no performance metrics and no wisdom to measure success and apply to future programs.

Bottom line: A lot of dollars, resources and time are wasted as results fall dramatically short of potential. But there is a more efficient, cost-effective way to run cleanup and marketing initiatives that will generate higher returns.

Market Segmentation and Testing Predicts Success

While traditional cleanup and marketing initiatives take a freestanding flat file approach, relational segmentation links multiple customer and prospect databases in a relational manner.

The underlying assumption is that various "cubes," (groups of like companies) can be tested with differentiating characteristics to determine the most valuable segments, and the knowledge can be predictively applied to generate higher return on future programs.

Steps include the following:

- Identify discriminating characteristics among the databases and lists.
- Segment the lists into small homogeneous cubes, or layers, of like companies.
- Conduct tests to profile and uncover opportunity in the cubes.
- Analyze cubes to find high-return segments and rank them as separate sub-markets.
- Use this intelligence to fully fund the right model for future programs.

The table below takes ABC Software's three databases and relationally segments them into five cubes for testing and analysis.

Setting Up Cubes for Testing		
Test Protocol	**Predictive Variable: Maintenance**	**Predictive Variable: No Maintenance**
Match 2 of 2	**Test 1:** C2 Maintenance customers *and* P1 Prospects	**Test 3:** C1 License-only customers *and* P1 Prospects
No Match	**Test 2:** C2 Maintenance customers	**Test 4:** C1 License-only customers
		Test 5: P1 Prospects

While databases are being tested in this example, any of the following can be tested with cube analysis:

- SIC codes
- Revenue or number of employees
- Annual growth percentage
- Decision-maker level

- Geography
- Offer (price, bundling, terms or delivery mechanism)
- Media (telemarketing, direct mail, email or print ad)

The table below depicts marketing response rates for five equally sized test cubes. This presents a dramatically different picture from traditional single-database marketing response rates.

nBase Marketing Equally Sized Samples					
A. Cube test	B. Sample size	C. Cube lead rate	D. # of leads	E. ROI option 1	F. ROI option 2
Test 1 C2 + P1	200	9%	18	32 leads or 64% of results with 40% of spend	42 leads or 84% of results with 60% of spend
Test 3 C1 + P1	200	7%	14		
Test 2 C2	200	5%	10		
Test 4 C1	200	3%	6		
Test 5 P1	200	1%	2		
Totals	1,000	5%	50		

While a traditional program can only generate response rates for a single database, a relatively simple database segmentation and testing cube approach has revealed three segments, or test cubes—Test 1 (nine percent), Test 3 (seven percent), and Test 2 (five percent)—that generate returns equal to or above the aggregate average lead rate of five percent. This provides the market intelligence needed to fully fund and roll out programs specifically targeting high-return segments.

Also note ROI data captured in Columns E and F in the table. Column E, for example, shows that Tests 1 and 3 generated 32 leads, or 64 percent of the program's 50 leads, from 400, or 40 percent of the 1,000 prospects contacted. Similarly, Column F shows the top three cubes generated 84 percent (42 leads) of the total (50) with only 60 percent of spend. This information helps marketers balance return against investment and determine optimal program deployment and funding for future campaigns.

While the previous table shows cube results from equally sized samples, this model can be even more useful by predictively weighting test segments.

Media – How Multi-touch, Multi-media, Multi-cycle Processes Multiply Results

The second "M" in M_2O encompasses how you approach your market:

- Media channels
- Frequency
- Reach
- Calendar
- Audiences
- Creative
- Activity reporting

Marketing campaigns can establish brand image without the prospect sensing a direct touch from the marketer. Sales calls can be insistent enough to irritate. Good lead nurturing falls somewhere between the two—enough contact to engage but enough space to respect the demands on a busy prospect.

The trick is to know how to balance the contacts between both timing and type of outreach. Mixed media programs that use a combination of quality outbound calls, voicemail messages, email and direct mail, optimally scheduled for greatest effect, are the most effective use of marketing dollars.

A senior executive at a well-respected analyst firm once stated:

"Many tech marketing departments are mere arrays of disparate tasks and uncoordinated contractors. I've been to a dozen or so firms in the last few months where the basics, like positioning statements, are so widely disparate that you wonder if they ever even talk about such things.

"Many of these groups deceive themselves because either they have won some award for a tiny part of the marketing mix, or, no thanks to their efforts, the company's overall success in the market to which they sell is increasing."

Harsh words. This part of the book speaks to marketing managers and their departments that seem to lack focus, have an inability to articulate a unique selling proposition and spend very little time thinking outside the box.

Every day a large percentage of leads are abandoned by sales simply because the prospect did not respond to a few, single-channel contact attempts. Salespeople generally do not have the time or patience to make the multiple touches, which can run from as few as eight to as many as 30 or more, to identify, qualify and nurture prospects to a point of sales readiness. Even immediate-need opportunities can take as many as a dozen attempts by sales to become effectively engaged.

A multi-touch strategy also allows the prospect to be contacted in his or her preferred manner. Most busy decision makers are not willing or able to arbitrarily pre-empt their business day to respond to a telephone sales contact, but can reply to an email or voicemail at their convenience and schedule a time for follow-up. Some prefer the anonymity of email; others are more comfortable with the personal appeal of voicemail. A combination, properly timed and executed, opens all channels of communication and thereby opens opportunities.

Actual interview I conducted with a technology company marketing director (MD):

DM: Describe your market.
MD: We sell to C-level executives in industries where excellent field service is integral to their operational and strategic goals.

DM: What is the solution?
MD: Our solution extends beyond ERP to the enterprise. Our solution covers everything from supply chain management, back office and customer and field services to sales automation.

DM: What is the buying process and what is your average deal?
MD: The sales cycle is relatively long with multiple decision makers involved. Our average sale is about $250,000.

DM: You mentioned that you are about to do a marketing blitz. What exactly are you doing?
MD: We are about to mail out 20,000 postcards.

DM: [pause] I'm speechless.

I call this particular conversation "Interview with a Vampire." Why? Obviously, marketing campaigns like these suck companies dry of marketing dollars.

Historically, database marketers have expected to increase their results by six to eight times when following up a direct mail or email campaign with a single phone call. But what you may not know is that stopping at that single touch can leave substantial business—half or even more—on the table for competitors to grab.

It's true. Traditional one-and-done advocates touch customers just once and then move on to the next big marketing initiative. That is extremely ineffective compared to campaigns that integrate multiple media and touch business prospects repeatedly. Multi-touch builds familiarity with busy decision makers and increases the potential of impacting them when the business need for solutions is high.

Throughout the years I have collected data while working with scores of clients and working on over 100 separate direct-marketing programs. As part of this, I tracked the number, frequency and type of touches performed and corresponding response rates. Analysis revealed that unless you are reaching prospects with at least nine individual touches—including a minimum of two email messages—you are not achieving the results you could.

Why nine? Well, that's the number of touches—delivered over a period of time through a combination of quality outbound calls, emails, voicemail messages and direct mail—needed to achieve the greatest level of response.

You can think of a traditional one-touch campaign as being a single dart thrown at a target—your prospect. A multi-touch, multi-media campaign is like a lot of darts being thrown at the target over an extended period of time. Such an approach boosts your chances for contact and helps to keep your solution top of mind until the timing is right.

Multi-cycle Amplifies Responses

In addition to multi-touch, multi-media approaches, there is additional benefit in implementing multiple cycles for high-touch marketing campaigns.

The initial contact cycle—the first time that you touch your market with a combination of nine phone calls, emails, voicemails and direct mail—will yield only 40 to 50 percent of the total opportunities. Continuing to touch the same prospects with the same multi-media, multi-touch strategy on a regular basis can identify other opportunities existing within the market.

In fact, lead rates from the second and subsequent touch cycles can generate anywhere from 120 to 210 percent of the initial lead rate. In most B2B markets return does not support the investment after the fourth or fifth cycle (and this can easily be tested and measured).

In other words, there is a point of diminishing return. The most effective way to cover prospects after the fourth or fifth cycle is through periodic email and/or direct mail—leaving the door open for them to make contact with you whenever they are ready.

Voicemail, Email Reach Busy Decision Makers

Contacts responding to voicemail or email have comprised close to 30 percent of all leads generated for most of my clients over a period of years. Perhaps surprisingly, however, the most frequent responders to voicemail and email have been the more senior-level decision makers such as C-level and senior VP-level executives as compared to lower-level managers. Senior-level executives are 2.5 times more likely to respond to a voicemail or reply to an email than are their subordinates.

Offer – How Speaking to Buyers' Pain Points Can Help You Leapfrog Ahead

The "O" in M₂O refers to the relevant offer, or message, you bring to the market:

- Corporate/solution/product/service positioning
- Segmented messaging
- Sweet spot definition
- Objections and strategies for addressing
- Potential messaging enhancements
- Competitive context
- Industry intelligence

How much should sales representatives talk about their product or solution? As little as possible. Effective salespeople know that good prospects sell themselves by talking about their particular business challenges, opportunities on the horizon, and emerging issues that will affect business goals. Asking the right questions and then listening carefully to direct further discussion uncovers pain points that are most likely to motivate purchase. When the prospect's needs are understood and can be matched to the benefits of a client's product, the sales-nurturing process can leapfrog ahead. Testing messages and offers such as guarantees, discounts and extended financing within market sub-sections can result in powerful learning and increase campaign results dramatically.

What remains imperative is that contacts, whether direct or remote, be made in a professional manner, in accordance with best practices gleaned through market experience. Most of the time, these contacts will establish the prospect's first active impression of the company, and the person making the contact must be assured, professional, approachable and credible. This won't happen by accident. Training, constant coaching, a proven process and a thorough knowledge of the client's offer are crucial to developing trust and purchase interest. In addition, results should be constantly reviewed to assess the best strategies for each client, each product and each target segment.

A friend of mine owns a company, The Content Factor, that specializes in content development, messaging and positioning for B2B technology companies. He publishes something called "The Jargon Quiz" on his website. The quiz does a good job of highlighting what is wrong with the way companies articulate their offers.

Here is one example:

"XYZ Company is the global leader that brings ingenuity to the places where people live, work and travel. By integrating technologies, products and services, we create smart environments that redefine the relationships between people and their surroundings. Our team of 140,000 employees creates a more comfortable, safe and sustainable world through our products and services for more than 200 million vehicles, 12 million homes and one million commercial buildings."

What does this company do?

- Make fuel cells, hybrid electric-gas technologies and other renewable energy systems?
- Install integrated, large-screen TVs and beer kegs?
- Provide green engineering and design services?
- Make thermostats, fire detectors, auto batteries and other equipment?

The answer is the last choice—but who would have ever guessed from the elevator pitch?

The point is to make sure you are speaking clearly to your audience so that they know what you are selling and, if they have a pain or interest, how they might benefit from your product or solution. If this sounds simple, you better believe that it is not.

Before diving into offer construction, let's take a look at what motivates buyers to buy:

- Fear of loss in the current situation.
- Perceived risk of a deteriorating situation.
- An opportunity to improve the situation.

The first of these three is the easiest to sell into. I always tell salespeople to continue to ask questions until they reach the first or second condition as selling to the third condition is selling into a rainbow and very difficult. Many No Decision outcomes in sales have to do with selling to someone who is always interested in learning how to improve, but has no real motivation to do so.

A couple of stories told by a trainer I once worked with will help your understanding of the conditions of need and their importance.

He asked his audience to think about two scenarios:

Scenario #1: It is 2 a.m. and cold and raining outside. Your telephone rings, you wake with a start and it is your next-door neighbor on the telephone. He says: "There is someone in your driveway and I think he is trying to give you a tire." You might mumble a few unintelligible phrases into the telephone, hang up and go back to sleep.

Scenario #2: It is 2 a.m. and cold and raining outside. Your telephone rings, you wake with a start and it is your next-door neighbor on the telephone. He says: "There is someone in your driveway and I think he is trying to steal one of your tires." You are likely to jump up, look out the window, call the police and go outside to protect your property.

The first scenario is an example of an opportunity to improve the current situation and the second scenario is an example of fear of loss in the current situation. The huge difference in motivation to respond in the two scenarios is as true in the real world as it is in these examples.

Understanding that there are conditions of need and that not everyone is in a fear of loss position (as an example) helps when you are creating messages for your target. Know what motivates your potential buyer and be a more successful marketing and sales executive.

There is a simple but effective way to test your company's messaging. Ask every possible stakeholder to answer the following questions:

- Who is My Company?
- Who is My Company's target audience?
- What problem does My Company solve?
- What is My Company's category?
- What benefits does My Company's product or service offer to the market?
- What is the competitive landscape?
- How is My Company different?
- What is the objective of this offer?
- What is the scope (from a dollars and time invested standpoint)?
- What is the timing?
- What is the budget?

Once that is complete, get someone to combine the answers and identify discrepancies (large or small). Then the most senior executive in the company should deal with tie-breaker issues—remember, nobody ever built a statue to a committee. Be bold and hold the team accountable for the decisions made around these questions.

Enough About Me…What Do You Think About Me?

The closer you are to the solution the more you need to worry about writing for the potential client rather than writing for yourself or other employees of your company. There is an exercise in sales training called "The So-what Exercise." It focuses on layering benefits for as long as possible until you reach one or more of the ultimate benefits.

The ultimate benefits are:

- Save money
- Save time
- Improve a product or service
- Save lives

Benefits are, ultimately, why anyone buys anything for their company. While you cannot simply say "Buy from ABC Company and SAVE MONEY," the reason why anyone buys from ABC Company will be to save money (or one or more of the other ultimate benefits). The key to using ultimate benefits though lies in linking differentiators to the most significant ultimate benefit so that the reader sees why buying from your company will provide a benefit and why your company is different.

As an example, one might link together the following: A strategic approach to planning, experienced staff and multi-touch/media and cycle processes will allow XYZ Company to cover more of its market more effectively and will focus the company's field sales force on the very best opportunities resulting in higher close rates and, ultimately, higher profits (more money).

The other side of offer development has to do with WIIFM (What's In It For Me). There are business reasons why people buy things for their companies and there are also personal reasons why people buy things for their companies:

- It's their job
- Recognition
- Security
- Compensation
- Self-actualization

When marketing (and selling) to buyers, it is important to understand not only why they might buy on behalf of the company but also what might motivate them to buy for their own personal reasons. Michelin® used to do a great job of marketing and selling to consumers. Historically, their tires were perceived as superior in quality and, hence, improve the product or service (great ride for more miles) AND they used a cute baby (riding in the center of the tire) to appeal to a parent's need for security. So the message was that smart consumers buy Michelin tires—for quality and to make loved ones more secure. I don't know why they stopped using this approach.

Most companies focus more on features and less on benefits; this should be the first place you look to improve messages and offers which will, in turn, increase and improve leads.

CHAPTER 7

What Doesn't Work When It Comes to Lead Management

There's an old expression that even a man lost in the woods knows where he wants to go. You may be lost in the woods, but know you must fix the problems that are causing the battle for success that is being fought between marketing and sales. It is time to understand what works, what doesn't and what to do about it. We just reviewed what works, but it is as important to review what does not work and why.

Kurt Vonnegut defined the term "granfalloons" in his book, *Cat's Cradle*, as follows:

"A group of people who claim to have a shared identity or purpose, but whose mutual association is essentially meaningless."

_____

Does this sound like the relationship between marketing and sales in your company?

Symptoms of the Lead-Quality Problem

One or more of the following conditions probably exists in your company today:

- Leads are delivered to sales with little, if any, specific lead-by-lead feedback.
- Marketing's objective defaults to quantity and cost-per-lead because there is no other way to measure or report on return.
- Forecasts are consistently inaccurate.

Your company is unique if some or all of these conditions do not sound familiar. The challenge is not so much in recognizing the conditions as fixing them. The common denominator in the problem is sales.

Sales representatives frequently do not value marketing leads. Producing great leads without any communication with sales and without differentiating those leads will not create different behavior. Also, sales representatives do what you pay them to do, not what you want them to do. So basic changes in forecasting that relate to compensation are always required if you want to tighten up the forecasting process.

Once your sales team has been trained to recognize that the leads generated thoughtfully, using a multi-touch, multi-media, multi-cycle approach, are more valuable, I recommend that they put 100 percent of these leads directly on their forecast with a 10 percent confidence factor at the average selling price. Taking a lead off the forecast should require a careful and specific level of oversight by senior sales management. This process is the only way to put teeth into the forecast and the demand creation process.

To help in the process, it is necessary to audit each lead and report back to sales and marketing on the effectiveness of lead follow-up. Reports generated from this auditing are among the most effective tools your company will ever receive from sales and marketing.

Marketing departments in most companies are a whirlwind of activity. So much activity—and often so much money burned. What are the results? Are you satisfied with the level of return on your investments in marketing and sales? Do you feel that there must

> **Which of the following is true?**
>
> A. Appointments are better than leads.
>
> B. A trade show lead is better than a cold call lead.
>
> C. Sales reps should work every lead marketing sends to them.
>
> D. The check is in the mail.
>
> E. None of the above.
>
> Answer: E

be gaps in the process between marketing and sales? If so, you are not alone.

There are a lot of reasons why there are gaps between marketing and sales. None is more costly to your company than spending money on "leads" that are not really good prospects, or creating good leads that are never followed up. Both happen every day at most companies.

There are two truths that are being ignored by many companies today, and it is costing those companies a lot of money:

Truth #1: Low-level leads created by trade shows, web hits, inbound calls and junior telemarketers usually lead to clogged-up pipelines and do not end up producing forecasted revenue.

Truth #2: Putting a good salesperson in front of a bad prospect does not yield cost-effective revenue.

Without professional filtering, most demand creation programs yield the following results:

As painful as it is, most senior sales and marketing C-level executives agree this is the situation in their companies.

Demand creation programs that include multiple iterations of segmentation, email, direct mail and telephone contact with continuous evaluation of each potential prospect opportunity yield the following results:

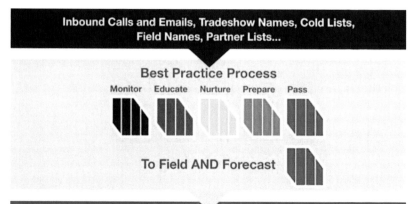

To make leads stick involves staying in communication with sales so that each individual's needs are met—as long as those needs are consistent with the needs of the company. Specifically, hungry representatives need the spigot turned all the way up, while representatives working on the final stages of several deals will simply squander leads that do not meet their time window.

Measuring Marketing Success Based on Cost-per-lead Kills Companies

No doubt one of the biggest problems with the management of sales leads today is that more and more companies base lead-generation buying decisions entirely on cost-per-lead. As an example, throughout the first decade of the new millennium many large companies, including a $1 billion-plus software company that has been one of my clients for years, have needed so many leads for so many resellers with so little budget that they have reduced the maximum cost-per-lead to a number so low that the only way to create the so-called leads at that price is to outsource the lead generation to India, the Philippines or Russia. Resellers complained about lead quality as soon as the process was taken offshore. Unfortunately, those complaints do not seem to matter because the decision isn't being made based on the quality of leads. Nor is it being made based on results or ROI. Instead, the decision is being made solely on the basis of cost-per-lead. Does this seem like a mistake? Yes! What are the results? In reality, no one knows. Field sales forces and resellers (or other descriptions for channel partners) are so conditioned to expect poor quality leads that they ignore most of the leads they get anyway.

There are two factors that make a cost-per-lead decision a recipe for failure:

Factor #1 – Conflict of interest: One department within a company is responsible for setting lead quantity objectives. Another department sets the budget. Yet another group is responsible for creating and executing a plan that provides the required number of leads within the budget. The department executing the plan has two choices. They can find a solution to create leads at the desired price, making senior management happy and thus earning their bonus. Or they can ascend to Maslow's highest level on the hierarchy of needs (self-actualization), provide the quality of leads necessary for success (albeit fewer than mandated), make management unhappy, miss their bonus, yet have the warm and fuzzy feeling that they have done the right thing. Which option do you suppose they choose?

Factor #2 – Communication barriers: Historically, overseas-outsourced solutions haven't been able to effectively provide high-end, quality leads. Customers calling for tech support or customer service are willing to put up with a certain amount of inconvenience—including some difficulty in communication—in exchange for the solution to a problem. But senior executives, who are being contacted for the purpose of qualifying them and their company for an expensive, complex solution, will not tolerate any inconvenience or communication challenges.

Companies are outsourcing to overseas or other low-cost providers simply because they are less expensive options that can produce the pre-defined number of leads companies want without regard to quality. The decision to use these providers has nothing to do with results, and it is killing companies today.

Demonstrating How

Allow me to demonstrate the fallacy of measuring the success of lead-generation programs solely on the basis of cost-per-lead:

Prospecting Campaign Summary	Example 1	Example 2	Example 3
# of companies	1,000	1,000	1,000
Required # of contacts/company	3	2.5	2
Expected touches per prospect	5	5	5
Total touches	15,000	12,500	10,000
Touches per day	100	100	100
# days required	150	125	100
Fee per day	$500	$500	$500
Number of leads per week	2.66	3.2	4
Fee per lead	$940	$781	$625

The fee-per-day is based on a fully loaded, full-time equivalent with a base salary of $50,000; upside based on results and includes benefit load, occupancy expenses, training costs, and supervision and technology costs. This assumption generally holds true whether you are using an inside sales group or outsourcing.

Over the past almost 20 years, the average cost-per-lead for a relatively complex sale (hospital revenue management solution, ERP, BPO consulting, etc.) has ranged from $750 to $1,500—and these programs returned excellent ROI. Assume, however, that you are working in a company that has been forced to evaluate and reward marketing on the basis of cost-per-lead and that the company mandates that cost-per-lead be $350.

Even in the best-case scenario, you only have two options:

> **Option 1:** Reduce the base salary for the individual creating the leads from $50,000 to $28,000.

> **Option 2:** Increase the number of leads required per individual per week from four to seven.

Which of these scenarios do you want to bet your company on? Most reasonable executives agree that Option 1 is unlikely. You cannot buy the labor required to accomplish this task for $28,000 per year or $13.46 per hour.

To increase the number of leads per week from four to seven, one would need to accomplish one or more of the following:

- Increase touches from 100 to 175 per day (impossible unless you can find opportunities without actually speaking with anyone).

- Lead rates would need to increase from eight percent to 14 percent (the 10-year average across a wide variety of products and solutions is five percent—14 percent is unreachable).
- Instead of talking to two line-of-business contacts per company, you can get by talking to 1.14 contacts (obviously impossible).
- Why waste five touches on every contact? You can really get by with just 2.85 touches (if you ever had to call a close friend more than a few times to schedule lunch you know why you won't reach a busy executive with just a few calls).

The reality is that leads cost what they cost. The market is relatively efficient. Lead-generation firms can no more overcharge companies for services than companies can significantly reduce the cost of maintenance services, as an example, without a substantial decline in actual and perceived value on the part of its clients.

Is it possible to create high-quality leads to support a field sales force selling a $100,000-plus solution for $350 per lead? Frankly, no.

How Much Should a Lead Cost?

I just covered how companies should not measure lead-generation programs on a cost-per-lead basis—but how much should a lead cost?

Your cost-per-qualified-lead is higher than you think! Virtually every aspect of our lives is counted: Everything from the calories we consume (too many), to the steps we walk (too few), to the number of tweets we send in a day.

Businesses are no exception. Supply chain statistics, number of days of inventory in stock, A/R aging and hundreds of other statistics are sliced and diced every day. On the top line, salespeople have quotas, marketing people have budgets and executives are frantically driven by quarterly results. With all that measuring going on, however, the most essential element of the cost-per-sale is largely unknown.

The Gap Between Marketing and Sales

They may be putting a pleasant face on it in your company, but salespeople seem not to understand marketing people very much, and vice versa. Salespeople complain about the quality of leads produced. Marketing complains that they never get feedback on leads, and that the field fails to follow up the good leads marketing creates. Unfortunately, both sides are right.

The fact is, fewer than seven percent of leads passed to sales by marketing should be. That means sales must contact 100 companies to find a handful of real leads. And that's a problem. Great salespeople (often called "hunters") are generally not great prospectors (or "beaters"). So when marketing sends 100 leads out to a hunter, it's likely that none of them will be followed up. If a beater gets hold of them, there's a better chance opportunity will be found—but of course, it won't be effectively sold.

Even when a sales representative takes the time to plow through a stack of leads and finds a good one or two, they're not very likely to pass credit along to marketing. So from marketing's perspective, all leads end up in a dark hole.

As a result of this dynamic, companies default to buying leads for the lowest possible price. And they end up measuring marketing by quantity, not quality—a vicious cycle with numerous drawbacks. *What can you do?*

Know the Numbers

- You probably know, or can find, the cost of each campaign, and the number of responses each yielded. For example, a $50,000 budget might result in mailing 20,000 direct mail pieces, or inviting 21,000 individuals to a webinar.

- Being generous, we'll assume a one percent response so that the direct mail and webinar invitations yield approximately 200 and 210 responses, respectively.

- Alternatively, you could execute a multi-touch, multi-media, multi-cycle campaign for the same budget against 1,000 highly qualified suspect companies.

- A good rule of thumb is to assume that five percent of your addressable target audience will have an actionable interest in your offer. So we apply the five percent short-term percentage to the universes described above and yield 10, 10.5 and 50 short-term leads, respectively.

- The following costs per short-term qualified lead results: direct mail ($5,000), webinar ($4,762) and multi-touch, multi-media, multi-cycle campaign ($1,000).

My cost assumptions are consistently conservative. But if you don't believe me, calculate the real cost-per-qualified-lead for your business.

Overcoming Objections

The two most common objections I hear when discussing these concepts are:

- The calculations ignore the residual branding value of direct mail.

- We do a lot better than the numbers you have used.

How do I respond? First, it's clear in today's economy that brand, or image, marketing is reserved for companies such as Coca Cola® and Microsoft®—not the average business-to-business technology company. Regarding the second objection, as much as 85 percent of direct mail to businesses is either not delivered, or never read by the intended decision maker. Even companies that avoid common mistakes (such as using standard mail instead of first class) find that mail delivery and recall rarely exceed 15 percent. Email is even worse. Sadly, otherwise rational people feel they should enjoy a two-percent response on mailings, as though this is an industry standard. The reality is that the average B2B mailing will pull 0.25 to 0.5 percent—which drives the cost-per-lead even higher.

Recommendations

Calculate and agree on an acceptable cost-per-qualified-lead. Do not accept cost-per-response as a substitute. In our example above, the cost-per-response is $250 and $238 for direct mail and webinars respectively, but those numbers are meaningless. Only the cost-per-qualified-lead ($5,000 and $4,762) will provide you with a clear picture of your return on each program. Basing decisions on cost-per-response rather than cost-per-qualified-lead will result in cascading inefficiencies along the sales supply chain.

Finally, hold sales accountable for EVERY lead. Add EVERY lead to the forecast. Take NO lead off the forecast without sales management approval.

So how much should a lead cost? More than you think, but probably a lot less than you are paying!

The Fallacy of Appointment Setting

It has been written that the best scams are ones in which the victim does not know he or she has been taken. By the end of this discussion, you will understand how this comment relates to appointment setting.

Most companies have previously experienced lead traction issues. The biggest complaint heard from C-level executives is that they have historically had no idea whether or not leads were being followed up. In addition, they have had no way of knowing how effective the follow-up is on the few leads that are.

One tactic some organizations have used to solve this problem is appointment setting. A number of so-called appointment-setting companies have sprung up over the past several years. However, to call what these firms provide an "appointment" is a misnomer. They are really scheduling "appearances" and creating the illusion that these appearances are with qualified prospects.

In reality, appointment/appearance-setting programs unnecessarily add cost to the selling process without corresponding benefit. Here is why:

- The most logical argument against appointment setting is, ironically, at the heart of its selling proposition. The selling proposition is that someone agreeing to see your sales representative has to be more qualified than another prospect simply forwarded to you as a lead. The truth is that in most complex selling situations, anyone who agrees to see your sales representative for any amount of time, without additional preparatory conversation, has more time to waste than most senior-level executives. On the basis of guaranteed appointments large companies send their sales forces on expensive trips (whether across town or across the country) when as many as three out of five of those appointments are with no-opportunity prospects, and at least one out of five doesn't remember scheduling the appointment.

- Companies like yours typically sell complex, relatively expensive B2B solutions requiring the involvement of multiple decision makers and multiple levels of evaluation. Could an appearance with one person, without advanced discovery, possibly be the best first step with a new prospect in that situation? The answer is that it is not an effective use of resources at this stage in the process.

- When good salespeople sell, they like to know something about the person they are selling to. They would prefer to present in a warm environment rather than in a cold-call situation. If they prepare the audience right, their visit is like a discussion with a new friend. If they have to go in cold, all of the focus is on the presentation. The reality is, few of your field salespeople are great cold-call presenters and when put in this situation, they're not being utilized effectively.

- You can search career sites and find dozens of ads for appointment setters. They are usually headlined as follows:

  "Earn up to $2,500 per week setting appointments!"
  "Earn money setting appointments, no cold calling!"
  "Earn $100,000 per year part time, no experience necessary!"

Are these the type of people you want engaging your market for the first time? If you never get a second chance to make a first impression, how would you like that impression to be made by someone who responds to one of the ads above?

Appointment setting works for the appointment-setting company, but not for its clients. The reason? The sales force's behavior on very expensive appointments is just like its behavior on any other lead source. They follow up the first few appointments received from any new source, find little or nothing in the way of real activity based on a few calls to each, and then no longer call on any new "appointments" and do not make the "appearances." Since the guarantee from most appointment-setting companies only pays off if a sales representative makes the appointment, the appointment-setting company is off the hook, you have paid a premium for the appointment, the sales representative fails to make the appearance, and in essence voids the guarantee.

Unfortunately, the company using appointment setting has probably squandered the marketing dollars that might have otherwise uncovered real deals.

If you are deploying your sales force by appearance only, better look under the covers as to what is going on and what is closing before the money runs out.

The Downside of Blueprinting

Low-level blueprinting is another popular so-called solution that reflects sales' distrust or lack of regard for marketing leads. Companies are driven to low-level blueprinting in response to sales executives saying something like, "The leads are weak" (with apologies to Jack Lemmon in the movie *Glengarry Glen Ross*). They go on to say, "Just get me the names of the executives in target companies, and I will get in to see them. I just need some names."

Here's how low-level blueprinting works (and I use that term loosely). Low-level blueprinting companies provide specific contact names to the sales force, and sales follows up. If they have a name to cold call they can get the rest of the job done, right? Wrong! It just does not work, and there have been a number of careers ended in the name of major blueprinting projects.

Most folks who understand the sales mentality will understand why. It's not unusual, during any given week, for my company to provide a client's sales representatives with a fully baked lead at an extremely well-targeted company in the client's home city, and support it with a digital audio file as verification of the conversation, only to find out later that the sales representative and sales manager failed to listen to the call and questioned the quality of the lead. Why, then, would sales pick up the phone and cold call a list of executive names? The answer is they won't.

Blueprinting works if the objective is to scour the market for key contacts, collect email addresses and other contact information and use that information for proactive, multi-touch, multi-media, multi-cycle contact programs. However, when someone says, "Just get me a name and I will do the rest," I can assure you that it wouldn't be a good idea to bet the farm on the outside chance that this will actually happen.

I understand why appointment setting and low-level blueprinting are so attractive to sales and senior executives. Most leads provided to sales by their own companies are weak, or even worse, not real leads. Even after a company has gone to the expense of generating low-level leads, it can take 500 telephone calls to as few as 100 leads to find two or three prospects that are worth additional follow-up. Sales simply will not do that.

I sometimes joke that sales is not afraid of work—they lie down and go to sleep right next to it. The reality though is that most sales executives work hard. However, good hunters (closers) are not good beaters (demand creators). Low-level blueprinting does not work, as it turns field sales executives into glorified beaters. The more you try to make hunters beat, the unhappier they'll be and the more likely they are to move on.

Telemarketing Cannot Stand Alone

Most people would prefer not to be called telemarketers. Yet the phone is one of the strongest tools in the arsenal when it comes to business prospecting. The problem is that it should not be used as a stand-alone media.

One-call cold calling is part of what caused sales to give up on leads generated by marketing in the first place. Historically, silver-tongued telemarketers have used phrases such as, "If I could show you a way…" or "How about I just send you some information and have one of our sales reps call to introduce himself?" to produce leads with no traction. Ultimately the result has been unhappy salespeople, cost without revenue, and prospects who think less of companies because of the constant barrage by low-level, poorly trained and uneducated callers.

To create valuable leads, you need a high caliber of staff trained in sophisticated selling methodologies and knowledge-able about mixing multiple media (such as phone calls, direct mail, email, personalized web pages and other electronic media) to deliver your message effectively.

I hear it all the time: Smart, integrated marketing does work. I spoke with a senior vice president of global marketing for a large software company about this very topic. He explained that when he's sitting in traffic or at the airport, he listens to voicemails and reads emails. Sometimes it takes six or eight times to impact him, but, as busy as he is, he concedes that timely and logical messages do compel him to pick up the telephone and call a vendor who appears to differentiate themself with solutions to pains he is suffering.

The bottom line is clear: One-and-done campaigns should be over-and-out for companies seeking a higher return on direct marketing investments. Multi-touch, multi-media, multi-cycle campaigns will multiply your marketing results.

"We Can Do It Cheaper Inside"

While selling outsourced prospect development I run into a lot of the same objections over and over again:

"Our business is different."
"No one outside will really get our product and/or service."
"I don't want telemarketers calling my prospects."
"We can do it a lot cheaper inside."

I hear them almost every day.

The business models companies use to take their products to market have changed dramatically over the years. In the '50s, everything was sold over-the-counter or belly-to-belly. A two-tier approach for technical solutions was not used to any large degree until the early '90s.

Today, sophisticated marketers use two- and three-tier, inside/outside and outsourced support models extensively. They find that a targeted direct marketing approach, including multi-touch, multi-media, multi-cycle programs, produces the lowest cost and highest quality leads as compared to any other method.

Let's look at the objections and dispel some popular myths:

- *Our business is different.* Sales is sales. Every business is a bit different. However, people buy things to solve business issues based on the solution fit, the reputation of the company selling the solution and the effectiveness of the salesperson. I have personally run programs where everything from a $1,000 operating system to a $10 million solution was successfully supported by inside sales. Many of my clients started out feeling that their businesses are different and that telemarketing would not work for them. I proved them all wrong.

- *Outsiders don't get it.* The really good salespeople I know would not dream of becoming technical experts. If they get a buying signal in the form of a technical question, and they are talking to a buyer, they are likely to bring in a sales engineer. The sales skills required to effectively solve any business issues can be documented and communicated for any company. No solution is that hard to get.

- *I do not want telemarketers ruining my prospects.* This is my personal favorite. In fairness, our industry has created the image. It is hard to think about telemarketing without remembering a time when you have been interrupted at home by someone who sounds like they can barely read, much less carry on a two-way conversation. However, as with any business, there are specialists. And, just as you would not dream of building an electric plant outside your office building to generate your own power, you probably should not invest in an inside sales function to support your revenue objectives. Maintaining productivity and keeping turnover down, as well as training and managing this function, is a job that few people can or want to do. I recommend, should you have this objection yourself, that you visit several technology-focused, business-to-business service firms prior to writing off an outsourced approach.

- *We can do it a lot cheaper inside.* A fallacy. See next page.

Cost Item	Inside	Outsourced
Hiring	$3,000	
Salary	$60,000	
Benefit load (17%)	$10,200	
Commissions (at 100% of plan)	$20,000	
Management	$6,840	
Administration	$8,966	
Rent	$1,470	
Computer equipment per year	$1,750	
Telephone equipment and usage	$1,525	
# of hours worked per year	1,960	
Effective cost per hour	$58	$61.50
Difference		+6%

As you can see, it is slightly less expensive to do it inside. However, you must take the following into account:

Hard Costs	Soft Costs
1. Staff turnover and retraining costs are not factored into the "Inside" cost side.	1. Best practices are expensive and time consuming to uncover and implement.
2. Cost of training management to effectively manage the function is not included on the "Inside" cost side.	2. Management turnover on the "Inside" side will be high.
3. Technology investment is underestimated on the "Inside" calculation as nothing is included for ACD, eCRM and other software required on the "Inside" side of the comparison.	3. Inside sales often defaults to decentralized, inefficient sales "administration."
	4. Objective of management and sales on the "Inside" side is to get out of the call center.

Too, in-sourced inside sales centers are notorious for their relative lack of productivity. See the following table for an example of typical Inside vs. Outsourced results:

(Assumes one person-year of effort in both cases)

Deliverable	Inside	Outsourced
A. Dials (per year)	9,800	24,500
B. Completed contacts[1]	980	2,450
C. % Leads (short/long-term)[2]	5%	5%
D. Number of qualified leads (B*C)	49	122.5
E. % Closed	20%	20%
F. # Completed deals	9.8	24.5
G. Average deal	$250,000	$250,000
H. Total revenue (F*G)	$2,450,000	$6,125,000
I. % Increase in revenue		250%

1) Outsourced includes more efficient completion of companies driving more deals.
2) Over the course of a year.

Other Reasons to Outsource

One way to spot an effective manager is to examine his or her ability to delegate. Likewise, the one fast way to spot a fast-growth company is to see what support it delegates and how well that partnership works.

Most fast-growth companies that outsource save money and enjoy higher revenue growth than counterparts that do not. Here are more benefits to outsourcing sales support:

- Access to world-class capabilities
- Increased control of quality and productivity
- Improved company focus
- Reduced operating costs
- Reduced risk

Can you really do it less expensively inside? Probably not, and probably not as well.

CHAPTER 8

The Truth About Sales

In this chapter we are going to talk about obstacles related to sales success—some self-inflicted and some imposed by sales management or other senior management. First a few facts:

- *Hunters, beaters and farmers.* Hunters kill, beaters beat the bushes for opportunities, and farmers farm the fields for up-sell and add-on opportunities. Hunters don't like to farm or beat. Beaters can't hunt. Farmers don't beat or hunt—although many think they can hunt, and that is a real problem. Do you know what type of salespeople you're hiring? Are you expecting hunters to beat? When you look at your sales force do you find 80 percent farmers and 20 percent hunters? If so, you're not alone.

- *Sales methodology.* Most of the salespeople you hire to hunt today really do not know how to hunt. Methodologies such as B-to-B Selling®, Solution Selling®, Miller Heiman®, and The Complex Sale® can all be effective. The key is to integrate your selling methodology with reporting systems and to follow through and follow up. Event training simply does not work. A sales methodology has to become a way of life. If your sales managers tell you that it is not important to train because they "only hire experienced salespeople," you better worry.

- *Sales motivation.* Do you want to know why there is never any movement in the forecast? Why is it that there does not appear to be any progress until an account is either won or lost? The first and main reason, as I've said before and often, is that salespeople do what you pay them to do, not what you want them to do. Sales executives are driven by control, credit and compensation. All three of these elements are strong motivators that can quickly turn into de-motivators. Sales reps want credit for everything. They will deserve credit if you can motivate them to comply with a true closed-loop system that tracks prospects through the buying cycle (I suggest rewarding reps who do this). Sales executives will often hide the steps in the sales process between lead acceptance and close. They fear accountability and being blamed for a loss, so they provide little visibility (except for wins) unless they are forced to do so.

Many people feel that building a sales force is relatively straightforward—hire the best-qualified candidates, provide training and compensate for performance. It's a step-by-step course of action that basically any organization can follow. But is that all that is necessary to make a good sales team great?

The reality is that while these practices—hiring, training and compensating—are all fundamental to the sales management process, other steps are often required to elevate the sales team toward dramatically improved revenue generation.

Consider sales training methodologies. There are many popular programs out there, and the truth is that most of them work well enough in teaching sales representatives the mechanics of working deals and closing the sale. Why then, after engaging the sales force in such a program, do revenue numbers shift only incrementally, and then only for a short period? To this same end, why do exciting new bonus plans and other sales incentives often fail to deliver hoped-for results?

At a higher level, sales managers have six basic jobs and they generally fail at three of them:

1. Hire
2. Compensate
3. Train
4. Deploy
5. Monitor and Manage
6. Coach and Counsel

In addition to hiring, compensating and training sales executives, there are three additional—yet equally important—elements required to yield results once the first three issues have been determined. If hiring, training and compensating are the science behind sales, then deploying, monitoring and managing, and coaching and counseling are the art of sales. Managers who understand and manage on the basis of both the art and the science of sales can greatly impact the outcome of sales opportunities.

Sales Deployment

Most companies tend to deploy their sales resources in traditional ways. For instance, small and mid-sized companies typically assign sales representatives to geographic territories, such as by ZIP code, state or region. Larger organizations may also deploy salespeople based on vertical industries.

Here are some simple criteria to determine if your sales reps are in the right deals:

Is this a real deal?
- Is the application appropriate?
- Is there urgency or a compelling event?
- Is a purchase justified economically?

How do we stack up?
- Do the solutions fit?
- Do we have the resources to win?
- Do we offer unique value?

Can we win?
- Are we fighting or leveraging?
- Are we credible?
- Is there a formal decision-making process?

Do we want to win?
- Short-term margin and/or annuity sale?
- Risk/reward relationship?
- Strategic value of the deal?

While this works well from an organizational perspective, the downside is that it requires little to no critical thinking. In comparison, ideal deployment processes involve putting the best salesperson in front of the best prospect at the best time.

In other words, each sales rep is a unique individual offering a specific personality, skill set and background—and what works well in one situation might not work well in another. A key job of the sales manager should be to match the sales rep to the opportunity at hand.

Let's say Joe is your top salesperson. Does that mean he should work Company A just because it is located in his geographic territory? Maybe not, especially if another sales rep, Mary, has special knowledge of Company A's business and industry. Perhaps Mary even has mutual contacts with Company A's chief decision maker. In this case, Mary may not be the best sales rep in the department, but she is the best sales rep for this potential client.

Instead of simply sticking to hard rules about territorial divisions, sales managers should apply practical thinking when making sales assignments. Smart deployment requires looking at each case independently and assigning a salesperson based on knowledge and availability. Regarding the latter—remember the adage about striking while the iron is hot. If your best sales rep is currently fully utilized, it may be best to pass the hot lead to the next best rep who is available and has time to work it.

Monitoring and Managing

In theory, a salesperson's time can be broken down into units. With 40 hours per week in a four-week work month, it can be assumed that a salesperson will have 160 one-hour units during which activities can be accomplished. Some tasks may take more than one hour—such as visiting a prospective client's office—and some may take less, but it is necessary to allocate these units appropriately.

Ideally, the sales manager will help sales representatives prioritize these units so that the best opportunities get a disproportionate amount of time each month. It is also important that the deals that may close the next quarter be given the right amount of attention to move them along. Note that I did not suggest working only the hottest opportunities! Sales representatives and managers frequently invest in sales cycles that are stacked against them and fail to invest in longer-term opportunities that could represent more revenue and profitability.

In order to accomplish these goals, it is my experience that a sales representative should have visibility into no more than 30 to 40 accounts at any one time, and should be focused on a short list of just eight to 12 accounts each month. This should be broken down into four to six accounts that require up to 50 percent of the sales representative's time in that month, and four to six accounts that require about 25 percent of his or her time. Some longer-term opportunities can also be worked into the equation that need less time-consuming, multi-touch attention—for example, an email every couple of weeks, a handwritten note accompanying an article relevant to that account, or a phone call every few weeks to discuss something of interest to the prospect.

Utilizing time in this way ensures that prospects are continually being funneled through the pipeline, and that the sales representative does not focus too much time on shorter-term opportunities at the expense of those that are longer-term. Too often, sales representatives have so many opportunities that their mode of operation is to give each account on their radar a "lick and a promise." Spread too thinly, the end result is that not much of anything gets closed. Imagine if a sales representative had 160 accounts and tried to give each of them equal time. Clearly, he or she would not be able to do much for any one account: one phone call, one letter, one sales visit. The chances of moving anything effectively through the sales cycle would be slim to none.

By monitoring and helping to manage the sales continuum, managers can ensure better results.

Coaching and Counseling

Many people think coaching and counseling are the same thing. Not true. Coaching involves working with an individual who is capable of doing the job, but doesn't have the knowledge to do it properly. Conversely, counseling is focused on someone who has the knowledge for the job, but will not do it.

In other words, many sales representatives have the aptitude for sales, but do they have the fortitude and attitude to be successful? It is the job of the sales manager to figure out on which side of the fence each salesperson in his or her charge falls. Given that salespeople are driven by the three C's—control, credit and compensation—this can sometimes be difficult to determine. The only way to efficiently and effectively measure sales performance is by carefully monitoring performance against a set of objectives that includes, but is not limited to, closing deals. In other words, if a sales representative is assigned 40 accounts, and at the end of a quarter nothing has satisfactorily moved along in the sales process, then you can bet that the next 40 will fare no better.

For managers, coaching is time-consuming but necessary, and should be looked at as an ongoing educational process to help sales team members reach their full potential. Counseling, on the other hand, has a finite number of steps. Designed to elicit a change in behavior, counseling should be directed toward those reps who seemingly have the tools for better performance but for whatever reason aren't using them.

One can look at the importance of both coaching and counseling by thinking of the sales team as distributed among three unequal groups. Those representatives in the top section (about 10 to 20 percent) care deeply about staying on top. Those in the middle (60 to 80 percent) are satisfied with staying in the middle but do not want to fall into the bottom section. And those in the bottom are fine with staying there.

If counseling does not work with those on the bottom, in all likelihood they will be terminated. This will redistribute the sales reps and change the dynamics since the new bottom will be comprised of previous mid-level performers. These sales representatives will have a greater desire for improvement in order to boost their status back up.

This also indicates that a good manager should spend more time pushing from the bottom up, rather than focusing on the reps at the top to improve overall sales team performance.

There is good coaching and bad coaching. For example, if a company has invested in a sales methodology—say Solution Selling®—and the sales manager uses that methodology religiously, then discussions with sales executives will be around the following:

- Pain – Is there an addressable pain?
- Power – Are we connected to the power?
- Vision – Do we understand the power's vision of a solution?
- Value – How valuable is a solution?
- Control – Do we have any control over the process and can we win?

If, conversely, the sales manager ignores what was taught and manages the way he or she always has (as an example, by asking a sales executive to rate the chances of a deal on a scale of one to 10), then the training investment has been wasted and poor results will be the net effect.

Here is an example of a counseling situation and the four simple elements of a counseling session:

Steve is bright and affable—by all indications, he should be a go-getter salesperson. You've coached and motivated, and provided the proper training resources. Still, Steve repeatedly fails to meet quota and does little to fill the pipeline with sales opportunities.

Is Steve putting in fewer hours than he should be? Is he failing to follow up on what you know to be qualified leads? Is he a poor, unprepared presenter? The truth is, after a certain point it does not matter.

Many managers are unsure of how to counsel team members. But counseling can be completed in four clear-cut steps:

> No matter what you assign to sales representatives, they will find accounts that they feel are better targets. So rather than fight it, go ahead and allow the sales rep to add targets to his or her list. However, you must also let them know that at the end of the day—and assuming that the representative is not hitting quota—only movement among the list of assigned accounts is going to factor into performance evaluations.

1. Identify the problem.
2. Identify the resolution to the problem.
3. Identify by when the resolution must occur.
4. Specify what will happen if the problem isn't resolved.

Oftentimes, a situation goes beyond coaching to counseling. By identifying the problem and corresponding resolution, and setting a time frame for improvement, the employee has a concise understanding of the expectations and outcome.

Conclusion

Hiring, training and compensating continue to be primary building blocks for sales force assembly and development. However, it is easy to overlook these additional elements— deploying, monitoring and managing, coaching and counseling—that are critical to optimizing sales performance.

By adding these steps to sales force management, a salesperson's chances for success are greatly increased, which will in turn impact your company's revenue.

Questions to Ask and Actions to Take to Improve Lead Generation

10 Questions to Ask

As obvious as it might seem, there are some basic questions to ask about marketing spend, and you will be surprised at the answers.

Without taking a close look at what is planned for your company, division or department, you may be surprised later to learn that your company has executed low-yield marketing campaigns. To avoid that surprise, ask the following questions about each campaign:

1. How much will it really cost?
2. Is the objective clear: Are we looking to gain awareness, interest or response?
3. What are the expected results?
4. On what basis are those results expected (best and worst cases)?
5. Would you approve the campaign if you knew in advance the results would come in worst case?
6. What were the results of previous, similar campaigns? If the answer is "not very good," why is it being done again?
7. If a campaign has never been tried before, has it been tested? If not, why not?
8. How critical is it to do this campaign now?
9. What process is going to be used to qualify, distribute and measure follow-up on response?
10. When and how will you assess the results of the campaign?

If these questions set off red flags for you, then stop the spending carousel in which dollars are going out with certainty while resulting revenue is coming in with less certainty. The tendency of most managers is to keep the carousel going. They fear jeopardizing short-term sales if existing or planned programs are reduced or eliminated.

The reality is that this faulty thinking is costing your company thousands, if not tens of thousands of dollars. Keep in mind that you can always reinstate a campaign later, but money spent today is gone forever. Cash is king. Spend yours wisely.

I have outlined universal issues regarding leads. Prospecting for qualified opportunities is a problem in every organization, every day, in every region—including yours. But the challenges surrounding leads are not impossible to solve. All you have to do is dedicate some time and focus to making basic changes.

After asking these questions, be prepared to take action.

10 Actions to Take Immediately

Once you've asked—and answered—the 10 key questions, it's vitally important to take action immediately. Without prompt action, your entire organization is at risk—but not because individuals in the organization want it to fail. Organizations fail because members of the organization don't know what the real rules are. Organizations that are fenced in by strong boundaries thrive. Organizations that are run loosely fail.

Here are the 10 things you need to do to ensure your company thrives:

1. Provide strong direction regarding integrated market, media and offer, and then reinforce it with strong sponsorship of appropriate activities and campaigns. As basic as it sounds, we work with companies every day that do not follow through on this.

2.   Get strategically involved in the marketing and sales planning processes. You will be surprised at how many things are being done backwards.

3.   Make sure that each and every customer touch meets strict standards that support the direction you have provided.

4.   Stick to your guns. Once you've made a plan, don't change it based on a subtle market change or limited market research. Avoid a strategy du jour or knee-jerk changes. Stay the course unless there is a valid reason to change.

5.   Hold marketing accountable for quality and value; make the sales force accountable for quality feedback and results. Very few companies or executives are actually doing this.

6.   Insist on weekly reports. Few companies have so many prospects that the entire management team could not review every one of them (their environment, what they're doing, who they're talking to) in just a couple of hours each week. It's that important.

7.   The sales force is driven by the three C's: control, credit and compensation. Ironically, great prospect development programs are initially perceived by sales to threaten these three C's. That is why you hear the following feedback on leads: "No telemarketer can talk to the decision makers I have to reach"; "I was already in that account and already talked to that decision maker"; "The leads are really not worth what you are paying for them, just get me some names and I will engage the prospects." These are not destructive, conscious objections. They are a natural reaction to the historical state of affairs and, as such, need to be addressed transparently and aggres-

sively. Eventually, great salespeople become great users of quality prospect development.

8. Insist on training. Start with the basics. Insist on self-education and participation in local and national events. This is a high-payoff activity.

9. Do not set unrealistic expectations regarding time frames and deliverables. Everything takes longer than you think. Quick solutions may make you happy for the moment, but you will eventually pay a price. Don't shoot the messenger who is trying to do the right thing and not the expedient thing.

10. Check your ego at the door. If something clearly isn't working, cut your losses, make the changes and move on.

Final Words

If it was easy, they would not need us.

If competing was easier, it would probably not be as much fun. Shortcuts such as setting objectives based on the number and cost of each lead, or creating appearances for sales rather than real opportunities, are well-intentioned examples of decision making that oversimplify a very difficult process.

This faulty decision making is often fostered by an environment that is created by senior-level executives, marketing management and sales management. Here are the fundamental truths that I reiterate to every client in this situation:

- Executive and C-level management owns responsibility for providing high-level market, message and media strategic direction. If you are a C-level executive today, and have given your team the direction that "our market is the Fortune 500" or "we sell enterprise solutions" (as examples), then you may be partially responsible for gaps between expectations and actual results.
- Tight, vertical and geographically defined markets are always necessary. Always. If you do not have a handle on this, from a deployment and message perspective, you are wasting time and dollars.
- The strategic-level messaging most companies use does not work. If you cannot explain what you do with a simple story and/or analogy, you need to work harder on carefully crafting just what you need to say.
- Close to 95 percent of most marketing investment is wasted due to marketing's focus on short-term leads and failure to value and capture the long-term leads. Also, frequently lost is information about companies that are qualified, but have no immediate opportunity—valuable

information that results from the process of finding short-term leads. Gathering market intelligence and applying the learnings in the context of a thoughtfully planned nurturing program delivers significant return.

- If you have an inside sales group, it is likely that they are either glorified administrators, or making 35 or fewer dials per day due to other pressing issues. That means that for every person you have in inside sales, every day you are settling for 65 percent less productivity than you should. You can't afford anything less than a dedicated group of trained professionals focused 100 percent on prospect development.

- Sales management has six jobs: hiring, compensating, training, deploying, managing and coaching. There are ample resources for the first three, but the secret to more successful sales management is deploying, managing and coaching. The best sales rep, with an envious comp plan and great training, will fail if not pointed in the right direction (deployment, including providing true hunters with fully baked sales opportunities) and pushed (managed, including requiring compliance with the needs of the corporation regarding SFA or CRM), and coached as required when things are not going well.

- An advocate is someone who will, without prompting, speak well of you and your company—and in essence, help you sell. Initiatives to keep customers happy can help you make money. Since buyer's remorse starts the moment the deal is signed, the activities, events and programs designed to create advocacy need to start then too.

- Does your company clog the pipeline with low-level leads created by trade shows, web hits, inbound calls and junior telemarketers? Is your company spending a fortune buying "appointments" that are really "appearances"? If so, you need it to stop.

Now you know The Truth About Leads.